Stepping Through the Looking Glass

Life on the Other Side

By Candace Caddick

Brightstone Publishing

First published 2016

Published by Brightstone Publishing
7 Blackstone Hill,
Redhill, Surrey RH1 6BE
United Kingdom

ISBN registered to me, the author, under Brightstone Publishing.

British Library Cataloguing in Publication Data
A catalogue record for this book is available from the British Library

ISBN 978-0-9565009-4-6

Printed in the United Kingdom

Cover design: Emily Westwell

With Grateful thanks to my daughters Pippa and Heather Caddick for their invaluable help.

Books by Candace Caddick

Planet Earth Today: How the Earth and Humanity
Developed Together and Where We're Going Next (2010)

The Downfall of Atlantis: A History of the Tragic Events
Leading to Catastrophe (2011)

And I Saw a New Earth: The Future After 2012 (2012)

Guidebook to the Future: Practical Advice for a Changing
World (2013)

Stepping Through the Looking Glass: Life on the Other
Side (Jan 2016)

Acknowledgements

I would like to thank my daughters Pippa and Heather Caddick for their unstinting support for me while writing this book. I'm also grateful for the encouragement of my friends Alison Hopkins, Gill Hancock and Masha Odintsova-Bayles. A special thank you to the amazing Emily Westwell for the cover design!

Contents

Introduction

This book, the fifth I have written with the Archangels, helps us discover what it is to leave the old world behind and step ahead into the new. The Earth was reborn in 2012, took a brief moment to gather herself together, then ascended in September 2015. We no longer live on the same planet energetically, we are stepping through the looking glass onto a new world where we are more aware of the higher dimensions and magic of existence. The Earth is a planet of light that grows ever brighter.

The energy on Earth today supports not only change but also finding and making those changes; it does not support the continued patterns of our old ways of living. It's as if a light bulb has come on in a room and we can see clearly, where before a major part of the circuitry of our world was missing. Now the circuit is complete again. The battery has been plugged back in and is filling the world with energy, where we had been running on almost the memory of that energy. The energy we create in our small physical bodies through eating could not begin to replace the contribution from the planet.

The energy today is higher and thinner making it easier to move through, with less resistance to moving forward. The light provides the transparency to see clearly those things that have not been right and need to change, that are continuing sources of unhappiness. There are dramatic changes ahead that couldn't even be contemplated earlier because of the lack of light coming from the planet.

This book takes us through the parallels between our time and ancient Egypt, concentrating on the impact the Atlantean survivors made on life there. The Archangels include chapters on magic, to help us break free of out-of-date limitations through understanding and practice. A change has taken place in the way the greater human soul intends to use death. Death can be a tool for consolidation and a splintered soul can become stronger by retiring some souls from the planet while others continue to incarnate. And finally there is more help on the way as humanity pulls out all the stops to bring through new waves of advanced souls to assist us. It's the beginning of a new future where we mean to succeed and achieve our own ascension.

I have written four previous books with the Archangels and they always want to write about something new and not repeat any information. In the text I put the names of the previous books near subjects that are more fully explained elsewhere, to assist any reader interested in further reading. Writing this book, they would say "more about death, more about magic!" until all the information was in the text.

Candace Caddick

Part One
The Years of Transition

1

The Earth's Personality

THE EARTH started a new 26,000 year cycle in December 2012 and is remaking herself gently from the inside. If you were to make a papier maché globe around a balloon, pop the balloon and withdraw it, it would resemble the way the Earth was reborn. You have been living on this new planet ever since then and while she may look the same on the outside, she is now very different on the inside.

If the Earth was an uncaring planet she could have remade herself in such a way that all life here ended in an instant, before reincarnating as an entirely new planet. But she took the more difficult path of constructing the new surface to look just like the old one, thereby causing the least disruption to those living here. The new surface was constructed over a few years prior to 2012 so as to be ready on time. The elemental kingdom was busy with scaffolding and finer building work, and some of you may have noticed your pets staring out the window for hours on end watching all the activity. Of all the life present here, only humanity is unaware of the new planet Earth and what it means to them in their daily lives. On December 20th 2012 at about 18.20 GMT the old Earth ended and the new Earth expanded to fit inside her new surface. Finally people are heading for the finishing line following years of living their lives haphazardly. Whether they make it across the line to ascension or not remains to be seen.

When two beings love and support each other they help one another. Of all Earth's children, humanity is the one most in need of help to awaken to full consciousness and know their place on a planet full of living beings. Earth has a multilayered ecosystem where each species occupies a niche in an all-encompassing web. Sometimes human beings behave like two-year olds playing with others and simply saying "mine!" Not all human beings, but enough to make a difference to all the other people and species here. There are signs that this is beginning to change for the better, and there will be more changes as the years go by. The Earth assists by changing the energy here, and as a being of light she is pouring love into the human soul; however this is not something that is completed in an instant.

The Earth pouring light into the human soul is one of the key changes taking place over the next decade or so. The human soul looks like a cloud heavy with rain, with a mottled grey appearance. Not black and evil, but somewhere in-between dark and light. There are patches of light, and patches of grey and dark-grey. How will humanity ever lighten up enough to ascend into light? (This story of the planet and humanity ascending into light was covered in the Archangels' first three books: *Planet Earth Today, The Downfall of Atlantis, And I Saw A New Earth*.) The way the Earth will fill the human soul with light is fairly simple, by singing to us of beauty and love. What if we can't hear the songs? She is singing them anyway and they fill your soul with light just like blowing up a balloon.

This transitional period during the first few years of the new Earth gives humanity time to adjust to the way the Earth is expressing herself this time around, and people do need a little time to process the changes that are happening. In some countries, such as Egypt, change happened in a matter of months in 2011, and happened again in the summer of 2013 to bring the government closer to what the citizens desired, (although they are now once again being obstructed by a military government again.) Egyptians are one of the first modern peoples in the world to stand up for the alterations in their government they wish to see. Imagine everyone working for the changes they desire over the next decade. Some will be quicker than others, some will be more violent, but people will respond to the incongruity of their governments being built on quicksand when there is solid rock appearing nearby.

Your social institutions were once created by the masses of people living their day-to-day lives, when the people decided what was needed and created it for themselves. During the 1800s in the USA, farmers would contribute money to build a school house on one farmer's land and hire a teacher to teach their children to read and write. They were willing to work together for something they wanted. Much of the current discord is a result of the detachment of the government from the people, and the amount of taxes paid throughout the year to support programs that are unknown, or even completely secret. Citizens are still obliged to pay for them.

In the UK there is the chance to vote for an MP once every five years, then he or she follows the party whip and votes with the government or the party leadership. Their career and status within Parliament is tied to their peer group, and they are a step removed from the people who elected them. In some countries this control of government is so self-enriching either monetarily or ideologically for the party in power, that people have to take to the streets to remove them. It's an action of last resort to put your body in the line of fire, but it's done to bring about change.

Should citizens of other countries step in and support those who are protesting their governments? That depends on how you see these protestors. Do you see them as part of your own greater human soul, equal to yourself? Or are they nothing to do with you? How would you like to be treated if you were in their shoes? That is the only guide we will give because it applies in all situations: treat others as you would be treated yourself.

2

Present Day Egypt

E GYPT is a country with a long post-Atlantean history containing layers and layers of past civilisations that shape the lives of people living there. Egypt became a great civilisation after the destruction of Atlantis, and much of what was in daily use in Atlantis was imported directly onto Egyptian soil. These Atlantean descendants remembered enough to build the pyramids, but forgot the correct dimensions needed to focus universal energy deep into the ground. They were only able to store this energy above the surface in the pyramids and release it as needed to the surrounding farmlands. Egypt became a land of light and was like a little corner of old Atlantis for a long time. When their knowledge was lost or distorted they turned in the end to black magic, and declined into a rustic farming land with a top-heavy religion and government to support. Although this took place a long time ago, it is part of the make-up of Egyptians today. Incarnating in Egypt allows a person to experience what it is to be multi-layered in one lifetime. Even their leaders share these attributes. Being multi-layered allows one to hold many points of view at once, and helps to live a balanced life.

Egyptians live in a land that remembers the storage of universal energy in the pyramids and the magic of crops that grew effortlessly year after year. The ground under their feet is the outer crust of a living planet, and she nurtured the crops to grow tall and healthily. The memory is held there in the soil itself, and people are born and die living on top of it. They do not live in isolation from the Earth; they eat the food growing there every day and wear the famous Egyptian cotton on their bodies. All the religions that pass through this land add another layer to the people living there, there is more to life and memory than humans realise. If they could see the layers of time they would understand that all the Egyptians that ever lived are present today but divided by their own streams of time. The old linear Earth time is weakening, and the wisdom of all these people make a contribution in the current days. Because universal time is "now", these people are all present at once.

Let's look at time for a brief moment here as this has been covered more thoroughly in previous books. Time exists on Earth to keep it separate from the rest of the universe, but time is a local planetary institution. Universal time is now, and Earth time is linear with humanity focused on events. The Earth will rejoin the universe one day, and is already resuming the universal time of timelessness. The shell that protected the Earth from the universe broke up in early 2013 and we are all being exposed to timelessness now. The only previous experience many of us have of the vagaries of time involved the phenomenon of "déja vu".

In Egypt the pre-and post-Atlantean civilisations, the Pharaohs, early Christianity, and Islam are all present simultaneously and the only reason we do not see all these people and cultures is that we deliberately chose to wear a blindfold and not see the timelessness of higher dimensions. To see the ever-present now on Earth it would help to observe the way the other life forms here exist in all twelve dimensions (including that of timelessness) and how animals live from one day to the next. Today's Egyptians are busy with their own lives, but they are set in a very interesting and overlapping series of cultures. In some places on Earth the veils are thinner, such as in the Arctic, and it is easier to access the higher dimensions. Often these areas will be in wild and natural areas as opposed to cities, but Egypt is a place where because of human activities in the past, there is enough light to thin the veils and keep open the pathway to spiritual growth. Once the veils thin then they are easier to rip away and allow you to see more and more clearly. The veils have been slowly vanishing since 2012.

You have forgotten what it is like to see energy and live in twelve dimensions, but so many things that puzzle you now will become clear when there are no veils to cloud your sight. At the moment you have to rely on your instinct and intuition, and trust your gut feelings on which actions to take. Maybe your ability to feel what is happening will awaken before you are able to see what is going on. Your ability to *feel* is based on your soul (which many of you do not entirely understand), and your sight is limited at the moment to eyes and brain. Those of you who see farther into the higher dimensions are tapping into the enhanced sight of your higher selves, and have developed a closer connection with them.

3

Angelic Teachers of Light

EGYPT began as a fertile country along the Nile river, thinly settled by farmers. It became one of those areas where we Archangels could come and teach in a way similar to our methods in Atlantis. There we taught in settled areas whilst sitting on a rock and gathering humans around us. That way knowledge could be absorbed and passed through the generations from parent to child. Where people were migratory it was more difficult for us to have the same effect. Those who travelled continuously and slept outside learned instead from the stars about the greater universe. Families in covered huts learned less from the stars and more from our instruction. No one was abandoned, and all had the opportunity to learn from the stars that the world was part of something far, far larger. Although unimaginably vast, they learned that the universe was a place of light. In the case of Atlantis, an isolated civilisation on an archipelago, we were able to instruct the population to quite a high level of skill and knowledge. We taught them about the Earth and how to keep her healthy by constructing stone circles, and how to use the power and energy of the planet to enhance everyday lives.

Egypt developed differently from Atlantis because of its lack of isolation, and there were those who wandered in and stayed to farm, and those who continued on into the surrounding areas. North Africa was not then a desert, although it has been since the days of the Roman Empire. Decisions about land management can have terrible consequences, but also in the case of the Romans it was conquered land, and they cared less about it than their own homes. They stripped it of wealth and shipped the slaves, raw materials and exotic animals they found home to Rome, leaving an impoverished land behind.

Egyptians learned from us how to use the seasonal floods for growing food, and there was enough food for the number of people and animals there. The Nile itself flowed naturally and enriched the land; it was a blessing to have the river fertilise the fields. When you think of farming as hard work, perhaps shovelling and carting manure to the fields, these farmers used the strength of the Nile to fertilise their fields in the annual floods. They never had to grow enough food to feed the millions of people that live in Egypt today. The work was hard but it was not backbreaking, and they were surrounded by their families and friends. Evenings were spent under the African stars in a pleasant climate and they sang and told stories together. Whenever you have spent evenings like this, have you been happy? They always had enough of everything: food, clothing, family and happiness.

We taught them, and they began to understand why they were here, and why they were living on Earth. You are all here to experience being alive, and learning about life through your relationships with other people. Ultimately you are here to remember the answers to the larger questions such as who is God, why is the universe here and how did it get here, what is humanity's role? As Douglas Adams wrote so succinctly in *The Hitchhikers Guide to the Galaxy*, it's the ultimate question of "Life, the Universe and Everything." Some of you became fully conscious over the years and learned the answers to the above questions; these people are now the human ascended masters. They are not lost to you but still exist as part of the greater human soul. If they could learn the truth, you can also learn it. We write these books to guide you on your way.

The ancient Egyptians were discovering truth (which is a form of light) through joy, the stars, and by our teachings. Think of these books as lessons, where we give you information and you listen. We hope you will take note and begin to spend more time outside in nature where you come under the tutelage of the planet itself, the trees and growing plants, the insects and animals. The Earth is always present, but she can be more difficult to connect to within the cities. There is not only too much concrete in the way, but concrete is a human construction and carries the vibration of humanity, not the planet. She would not choose to cover herself in cement or roads. Her hills are like the moving waves, but they move so slowly you would not see them advance in many lifetimes. Ribbons of roads and even cities are being built on a moving surface. When your buildings were of temporary construction it didn't matter, you were able to leave and move somewhere else easily.

You can visit an area of rippling hills like the Welsh Marches, and see the wave pattern from the top of a high hill. There is no doubt that you are looking at the wave action of the Earth's skin. How solid is the Earth? She has an energy body that is as lively as an atom with electrons whizzing around the core, and yet her physical body holds a stable round shape for you to live on, thereby creating a platform for your feet. Think of your own rapid thoughts, some of them happening when you are sitting quietly. Are the microbes that live on the surface of your skin aware of your inner mental activity? Would you expect them to be? You know from biological science that there are many, many such small forms of life present on your surface and inside you. These successful patterns of life are repeated on and in your body based on the model given you by the Earth. You no more understand her complexity than tiny microbes understand all about you.

4

Learning to See Clearly

EARLY Egyptians lived out of doors for most of the year until the rainy season arrived and the Nile was in flood. It was easy for them to move to higher ground and build a shelter for those months. Living outside may sound similar to living like animals, but animals that run free are generally happy and look after themselves according to their natures. They take shelter under trees, in nests or caves, but they spend most of their time outside. They pass among the plant life and wildlife and learn from observation. More than that, their energy bodies blend temporarily with the trees, plants, animals and insects as they pass by. For a brief moment of time they are one. It is not so hard for them to grasp the concept of unity as it can sometimes be for you.

Many areas today are treeless, where once there were forests. Some of the deforestation in Europe and Africa was to do with the Roman Empire and the civilising of the Roman provinces into farmlands. The tribes that lived in the dense German forests were protected and comforted by the trees. Their energy had blended with the trees throughout their lives, and the trees were aware of them. Today humans are so invisible and without energy that they are able to enter a forest and cut down the trees, and the first the remaining trees know about it are when dead tree trunks are lying on the ground. (It sounds like one of those horror stories where members of a group are quietly killed one by one.) One of the advantages of practising Reiki or another healing modality is to become visible to trees. The human energy field becomes white and filled with energy, and that person can walk under the trees and be seen like a star. That's why one of the first things a person may hear from a tree is "I see you."

Wouldn't it be good if everyone's energy was shining and white? How can it be that there are so many people in existence with just enough energy to walk, talk and eat? They are biological bodies with little energy: and can it really matter that they are not shining and white? What would happen if the only people alive on Earth were full of energy and light? They would not wish to cut down trees, and the trees would then be able to teach greater numbers of humans about love. Trees are like fountains of love in wood form. Part of living on the new Earth is the ease with which you can find the right person to help you at the right time, and they are also able to find you. This is the way that flow manifests in your lives, and you become like the ball in a pinball machine pinging from one person to another, while they are doing the same to find you!

When you hear of something that upsets you, such as a new road going through a beauty spot or fracking for gas, who do you think has put it in motion? It is likely to be people with no light energy, and you who read these books already carry the energy of light. Never doubt that you can effectively oppose wrong projects. They do not contain the energetic strength to succeed unless there is no opposition. Everything changed in December 2012, and those people are old Earth, they can only succeed if you lend them your own energy. There has been an energetic power shift, and you have the strength to oppose projects that seem wrong to you.

We've been writing about people with no energy, but another way of saying this is that there are some people who have downloaded a greater part of their soul than others and this helps them to be filled with energy. If the splinter of human soul in a body is very small this manifests in the way a person spends their life. This is not to say that some people are less perfect than others, but that they have a different role to play. Perhaps the person or corporation that is instigating something "wrong" is doing it to call forth the best response you can give. Your actions will have come about because of their actions. You need to see all of existence as a spider's web, where a tug on one strand jiggles the whole of the web. It is how life is designed to be, as an interlocking experience. Right and wrong are shrunk to your own response and the way you use your life. Remember that you are perfect, and as long as you *always do the best you can*, you will finish this life having done that which you came here to do.

In addition to there being people with no energy, it also applies to man-made organisations, and there are so many of them from governments and business to hospitals and schools. Nations, cities and canals are man-made. They are not all going to vanish because some of them carry the right energy already, whilst others do not. When we talk about change, can you imagine a corporation that exists simply to make money with no intention of selling a suitable product? Maybe you can think of a few of those businesses right now. They are run by these "hollow" people who won't be reading this book. This leaves you the job of trying to identify what kind of businesses you wish to deal with daily.

In order to identify a business that is built along the lines

14

of the new Earth you have to release any notions about price. Often the cheapest price costs too much when you think about the workers in sweatshops. If you buy clothes or shoes that were made by child-labourers, then you are wearing clothing that carries the energy of sadness. You clothe yourself in this and never notice. It's like eating meat from a frightened animal: you eat the energy of the meat. You are able to feel this residual energy right now if you choose to, you simply have never tried before and this is the kind of activity that improves with practice. Buy fewer items and make sure they feel right to you.

Wearing the energy of exploitation and eating the energy of fear affects the goods and food as much as chemicals do. If you are making an effort to avoid chemicals in your life then you need to focus on what else goes into the make-up of the product. To start we recommend eating well and dressing in organic, natural fabrics. As you detoxify chemicals they will move out of your physical and energy bodies (chemicals have an energy signature, too), and as you become free of foreign energy and less adulterated with outside vibrations you will find it easier to use all of your senses while you continue to detox. One of the biggest blocks to your ability to sense and to channel other vibrations is mercury in tooth fillings.

How can anyone become this pure? Think of it as progressive, where you take steps towards detoxing with the goal of arriving one day with a clear head and body. It can take a few years but it is worth doing because toxins form some of the most elementary veils blocking what you were born to be. Not all the veils hiding the sight of the real world were made by others. There is only one major veil that was not put in place by humans and you are not ready to help remove that veil yet en masse, although a few of you removed it as individuals. (That veil hiding the fourth and fifth dimensions is described fully in *The Downfall of Atlantis*.)

Does it sound improbable that your higher sight will clear as you detoxify? You've changed a lot over the last few hundred years. There are many reasons for this, and one of them was the fear of letting others know what you could see. There was the threat of being labelled a witch, and being executed hanging over those who worked with the natural forces of the Earth. Think back to over two hundred years ago before the birth of the industrial revolution when there was clean air and water. You did not breathe in toxins or eat them. Your food was grown organically with manure from animals that were not fed on toxins or antibiotics, and there were no chemical fertilisers. Chemicals are a new development and have now spread around the world. Even those who live in primitive societies on Earth are carrying a heavy load of toxicity. There are also some areas of the planet, such as Bhopal in India that have been famously polluted by chemicals with resultant birth defects. In order to eat, these people had to work and live near chemical factories and put themselves and their children at risk. Humanity became sluggish and lost its higher dimensional sight when you ignored your intuition, while at the same time the planet became toxic. Even today it takes a brave person who sees fairies to admit they can see them.

Going back to the days before Atlantis to a time when the human experience on Earth was very new there were choices and decisions to be made. The most important decision was to play a game where humanity could not see the higher dimensions and was restricted to the lower five dimensions; the other decision was to be born here in a state of 100% ignorance of who you really are. Unknowingly, you began a lonely game of finding out what it means to be human. Many of you did this over the millennia and ascended. The rest of you are on a journey to join them in ascension.

5

Life on the New Earth

IN DECEMBER 2012 at the rebirth of the Earth, many people did not choose to continue their lives on the newly reborn planet. In the end less than one-third chose to step onto her surface. The rest are living on a planet that used to exist but is now gone, and they either can not or will not recognise it. They are alive because this is a gentle transition, but many of them no longer belong here. This in turn affects their life spans, as each person's higher self will now begin to bring the incarnation to an end. You can expect to see more deaths across all ages and income brackets from now on. While they are alive they will be self-supporting, that is they will not have the support of the Earth beneath their feet. They can also be supported by you and this is a question of judgement: who is worth supporting with your own energy? Yes to family members, no to some others. And yet, you will find some people supported by the masses for one reason or another. This is why we want you to develop a sense of detecting who has energy and who does not. In recent years some of these people show more and more signs of being ineffective in their lives. It is also possible to see a line-up on a stage or TV program and notice that some people have less energy than the background scenery made of wood. One way to identify who has not joined you on the new Earth is to stretch your senses out and see if you pick up zero energy with certain people. Others will feel like real people to you.

Try it at night in bed and count how many people there are in your house by feel (your pets will have energy.) Empty-nesters don't say "the house feels so empty" for no reason: you can feel the presence of your family.

There is a new pattern to death now, in the past it was like a river of coins where new coins pushed on at one end and old coins fell off at the other, which is still holding true for those who chose to come along with the new Earth. Now it is more like two rivers of coins side by side and all the new coins join the new river as in the past, but the other side is experiencing young and old deaths with no new coins joining the flow. Maybe you have been shocked by some people's early deaths, but we see them as those who did not but we see them as those who did not wish to go forward at this time. Not everyone does. But here is where it is different: those who die from the old Earth have finished their incarnations, and have rejoined the greater human soul for the duration of humanity's time on Earth. You will not meet them again until everything has changed and a new game has started for humanity. As in the aftermath of Atlantis, this allows the greater human soul to simplify and consolidate what has become a very splintered game, although Atlanteans souls splintered because of their damaging practice of cloning.

You have at the moment seven billion humans on the planet, far more than you require to learn who you are and why you are here. It's getting too hard for people and families to survive, and the living conditions for success have diminished so much that this game was stalling on the old Earth. When all you can think of is your next meal you don't contemplate Life, the Universe and Everything. Seven billion incarnate people have put pressure on the soul group by splintering the human soul to animate so many physical bodies. The number of people on the planet will decrease, beginning now, and their souls will recombine. First the full benefit of overcrowding will be experienced, even if it does not feel much like a benefit. You produced this many people so quickly for a reason, partly to learn why you don't want to do it again! There are reasons affecting climate, famine and fresh water that will implode on you first. Some of life's best-learned lessons come from mistakes.

This is the first time you have covered the planet in your own species, resulting in you taking more than your fair share of the living-space and food for yourselves. Previously you were content to live an agricultural lifestyle, and in order to experiment with high levels of population you needed to become more industrial. Your many scientific inventions have allowed you to feed and house more and more people. Questions were answered here: Could you create an environment that would allow you to expand your numbers to the maximum level? What is the maximum level? What are your lives like when the Earth hosts this many humans? What changes took place as a result of the high levels of people living here? What have you learned by moving en masse into the cities? How will you rebalance again? Your entire time here has been a series of experiments and explorations into what it is to be human and alive on Earth.

You are not the first beings to experiment with high population levels. In previous incarnations of the planet there were some who did exactly the same. Life is a learning experience, and you are approaching the end of your time for lessons. When almost everyone agrees that there are now too many people, the population will start to decline. The energy has already changed from increase to decrease and the physical manifestation will follow in a natural manner. First you will have some fresh water issues to deal with, as well as food and fuel. The shrinking of the birth rate has begun in some countries already, and in other countries it will begin in the next few decades.

Once the birth rate begins to contract there will be economic issues along the lines we discussed in *Guidebook to the Future.* If everything happens too fast there will be innocent people caught in the fall-out, or will there? This is where you can use your intuition for where to put your life's savings and investments. The difference between something having positive energy is very different from the blankness of no energy. You need to assess the existing energy to know if you have found a safe place for your money. The economic reality of the past fifty years will be far different from what is coming over the next thirty years or so. Invest in yourselves, in others, and in your communities. Wave goodbye to the multi-nationals and hone your intuition, you have to feel your way towards the truth and light. It takes practice but you do some of this already. "I didn't take the usual route home today and missed a giant traffic jam." "There was something about the offer that didn't feel right." "I knew if I turned left there I would find a parking space!"

How do you feel when you take a walk outside? Are you relaxed? Does your nose enjoy breathing fresh air, while your lungs fill with oxygen? Your nose can be quick to let you know when you are breathing polluted air, and you turn away and try to breathe shallowly until you are away from it. Some workers have no choice but must continue to breathe in the smoke or chemical fumes. Beaches carry the fresh air of miles of moving and churning oceans, and although ships can be very polluting they take up less space than cities do. The seaside breezes bring you the freshest air many of you will ever breathe.

Fresh air and ozone go together, and it is the disappearance of the ozone layer that demonstrates the health of Earth's atmosphere. Couldn't the Earth herself fix it? She could, but how would you learn about cause and effect or about being responsible for your actions if she did? Climate change has been confirmed by international scientists and they link it to human activity. Understanding this could help changes to be made in the way humans live and work and the way they affect the planet's climate. Earth is very fast at processing all lessons and helps you to move forward to new ones. Does she participate in climate change? Of course, and she is still helping you to learn by taking your actions and intentions and manifesting them into your reality. You create the thoughts and take actions like burning coal and oil, and she uses these to show you the results. You've been burning for a few hundred years and she is not repairing her atmosphere, she is allowing you to learn what happens when the air is fouled. You are still here, and she is now providing you with the home you indicate you want. We find it interesting to watch, it's like a tennis match. You hit the ball to her and she returns it to you with a spin.

Today there are whole societies built on quicksand, as the ones you established on the old Earth are no longer on a firm foundation. A building on quicksand will begin to wobble, sink, crack and fall apart. Humanity finds itself on quicksand at the moment, by some living on a vanished planet with no energy, while others make new lives on a new Earth. If you were standing on your feet and there were no longer any chairs or beds in existence, how long could you stand on just your own energy before collapsing? The old Earth ceased to exist and provides no place to sit and rest. This process of institutions and people standing upright solely on their own energy began when the Earth was renewed in December 2012. One by one everything that remains from the old Earth will run out of energy and begin to tremble and fall. Sometimes people and institutions look like they are sturdy and filled with sand, but now the sand is running steadily out.

How do you protect yourself from this type of collapse? What is it you wish to protect? This is the real question, and the answer will often be my house, and the security that I can look after myself and my family. Often it simply comes down in the end to "I'm afraid I won't be able to look after myself, that I'll be hungry and homeless." The people who read this book are going to see society-wide change in their lifetimes, and change from one way of living to another. We believe the changes will help people live happier lives.

We write these books to reassure readers, as living through this amount of rapid change can be scary. You may find yourself in a completely different life very quickly but we want you to think about what disappeared, and then what was new that arrived in its place. Were you happy? Did you know your family, children and neighbours? Did you play an active role in your daily life, or just go to work in order to earn money to live on?

When we've written that you should not lend your energy to anything that is falling apart right now we are speaking from a higher point of view. You've heard the term "don't throw good money after bad." In this case don't throw your good energy after bad, don't prop up something or someone with your own energy but use it instead to create something new for yourself. The best way to use your energy is for yourself and your own plans.

Once the changes have all worked through, and this will be faster in some countries than others, you will have new social structures that are built on rock. When you interact with them they will not require your energy as they will be stable and supported by the Earth they sit on. This is going to happen and your personal choice now is do you hasten their collapse by withdrawing your energy, or do you prolong them by trying to prop them up? Remember change is difficult at times, but once you have made the changes and started again it becomes easier.

The changes we are talking about are switching from actions that are not based on love for all, to living lives based on love. This means seeing the larger picture each time you act, until you see yourself as a small part of a very large web by considering first other people, animals and insects, then the planet and the universe. When you get to the point of knowing how you contribute to life everywhere and your own place in the web of life, you're finished with this game on Earth. As in a computer game you move up a level and continue to learn new lessons from a different perspective. That's what ascension is all about.

In our book *And I Saw A New Earth* we described how ascension will be for humanity and the Earth. The Earth organised a series of games that would take herself and the life on her surface to the next level, where as an ascended being she is beginning a series of rapid changes that we are living through now. In her original plan she contracted herself to a large number of souls, one soul for each species present on Earth today. This is an incredible number of souls, all the same size as Earth (we measure souls by the amount of life they have, and to put it simply, all souls are alive and therefore equal.) This new group of souls will ascend when they learn that they are all one and a tiny part of God, releasing their barriers to blend together. The new coming-together makes it possible to share all their experiences and knowledge, and grow in wisdom. This combined soul has gone as far as it can toward ascension, and it will wait for the Creator to draw this universe to a close. It will be a relatively short time until the entire universe returns to God, and the life experiences of all beings across the universe become a part of the Creator. Everyone will be Home, and there will be no more loneliness and separation, only wholeness and love.

In your own lives transition will take many forms, but if you choose to work with the energy of the new Earth you will find some parts of your lives have become intolerable. Like wearing a shoe that rubs, you will take the steps necessary to change your job, your home, perhaps your partnerships. You could have made these changes years ago, but now on a new, stronger planet you feel surrounded by energy supporting what is best for you. Is it best to earn a high salary, perhaps commute and work very long hours, and never enjoy life? These are the type of changes that have begun to work their way through.

A long time ago the Earth made a contract to host the human soul (contract in *Planet Earth Today*) in playing a game designed to see if they could find God from a position of complete unknowing. Humanity began a series of lives to see if somehow, as the years passed, they would realise that God existed and that they had a relationship with Him. This relationship seemed to take many forms and greatly depended on which spiritual teacher a person followed. Others found God through living close to the Earth and the night sky and learning about themselves as part of a greater universe. A few people and entire civilisations learned enough about themselves and their relationship to God that they finished altogether and are waiting for the rest of humanity to catch up and join them in ascension. The vanished civilisations of the Mayans and the Orkney Islanders are two such groups. All that is left of these advanced civilisations are their archaeological remains.

Mayans were descended from the Atlanteans; some survivors came ashore in the empty lands of Central America and put into practice everything they could remember from Atlantis. They also built pyramids similar to the Egyptian ones. You have to remember that those who survived Atlantis were not the pyramid designers from the central cities, but were fishermen and farmers from villages nearest the sea. All the Atlantean cities had become dangerous places by then and the people on the coasts were unwilling to cross the open fields to visit them. They concentrated on escaping the notice of the local rulers by living quietly near the shores. When Atlantis ended they took to their boats.

The Mayans were alone and living unhindered in their Central American location and were able to continue the best practices of Atlantis by living with the Earth and balancing her energy flows. They built pyramids in the correct locations, even if they were not the correct sizes. This helped the Earth connect to the universe, and helped the Mayans to live in an area with a strong incoming flow of universal life force energy. The light in this energy helped them learn and ascend together as a community, which is by far the easiest way to ascend. In a community information is exchanged and the growth of the individual is accelerated.

The Orkney Islanders, located just above the mainland of Scotland, were completely untouched by the events that happened in Atlantis. These islands are almost flat and treeless and they could see the stars and some of the universe quite clearly. The stars were so bright in their night sky that darkness was not fearful, and as they watched the other bodies of light they knew they were part of something far larger than their small islands. The lands around the Arctic Circle are set in the part of the Earth where barriers to the outer universe are the thinnest. It was easier for them to grasp their relationship to All There Is than it is for those who live under a thicker barrier and with too many distractions in their lives. The reason you have the Northern Lights is due in part to this thin barrier between the Earth and the outside universe.

These are two quite different examples of entire civilisations finding their route to ascension as a community, and there have also been many individuals over the years to ascend. They remain human, and they contribute their knowledge and experience to humanity. These human ascended masters and mistresses are available to those of you who have raised your vibrations high enough by practicing healing, such as Reiki self-treatments, so that they can be in contact with you.

You live in a world of possibilities where you can take individual actions and follow your own route to understanding, or like the Orkney Islanders you can learn together. It is much easier to learn together and ascend together, and you have become so lonely on Earth learning about yourself in solitude. Soul groups are one soul that has divided into many physical bodies, and any action that takes you closer to working together will be more effective and at the same time reassuring. Maybe you think no one shares your interests, but there is always someone who thinks the way you do. You are all chips off the same block, and you have your soul in common with the people you meet. You just don't recognise it at the moment. Each person has put up barriers around their splinter of soul, so which is stronger – the barrier or the core that is being protected? The core is the strongest, but some people never come in contact with theirs in a lifetime and live within the high walls that they've built around their hearts.

The home of the soul is in your heart, and it's the truest part of you. If you can drop your focus out of your chattering brains into your hearts you will feel that sense of recognition that comes when there are no more barriers between your physical self and your whole, higher self. Then you often realise what a lovable and special person you are, a genuine being of light on the Earth. For this reason we recommend frequent meditation to help remove all the barriers you've erected to hide behind. Knowing yourself allows you to meet others as your real self, and gives you a chance to become closer to them.

There is a division between what you expect and what you receive from life that goes back to the very beginning of humanity's time here. You came to Earth to learn more about your place in the universe, and the true nature of your being. The civilisations that developed where they could see the universe were greatly influenced by living with the stars. Every star has a signature energy and song, and these civilisations would have been aware of the unique song belonging to each of them. Listening to all their singing voices the people would have learned enough to ascend through the information the stars provided. The vibrations of the little planets in your solar system are small when compared to the great stars of the universe.

Today some lucky people live away from the city lights and trees, and can still see the stars. But you have lived for many millennia on a planet where the energy in the atmosphere itself is less clear in the dimensions above those of height, width and depth. There are fogs of darkness on Earth that dim your sight; are there any of you that know what the stars are singing today? Your energy fields around the Earth hold the anger and pain of wars and murder and you need to see through these fogs to see the stars more clearly. These fogs are created by mankind and are not permanent, but they influence you by creating an unenlightened environment. To create an environment of light requires individuals and groups to be healers to counteract the darkness. Darkness creates more darkness and violence, light creates more light and love. If you want to change the world then heal yourself daily and fill up with light. Light spreads as easily as darkness.

This is our fifth book channelled through this author, and in each earlier book we explained why we want you to get together in groups and form healing circles. We're not giving up with this message. It's how to change the world.

Part Two
Hitting Bottom - Ancient Egypt's Solution

6

A Civilisation Without Time

MANY OF you feel you have come close to hitting the bottom financially. People in the wealthy West have seen their salaries shrink compared to the increasing costs of living for housing, fuel, food and taxes. At the same time the funding for schools, hospitals, libraries and amenities have been squeezed and these are not as freely available as they once were in the local communities. In the UK there can be long delays for health care, and as the closest schools fill up many children are bussed further away, leaving them even less time to play. Library staffing levels and their opening hours have been reduced, and sports playing fields sold off to raise money for local authorities. Charges have been introduced for many services that were once paid for by taxes.

What does the bottom look like, and how do you know when you've hit it?

Before we go into current economics since the downturn of 2008, in this Part of the book we want to talk first about what happened in the past in Egypt. There's a lot of guesswork in popular books about timings and events in ancient history, and there is a straight time line to keep track of the known events. Early Egyptians managed to escape linear time for a greater part of their past by living in the now, by not giving each day a name and order, and by working with the seasons. The name of a day didn't matter, it was just "now."

Because of this day-to-day living there are a number of events that can't be pegged to a time line. As an illustration, imagine a cloth bag filled with events from those days hanging below the familiar time line. We are going to take you into that bag and explore some of its contents, zigzagging around irregardless of human Earth time. This is where much happened that you may have an inkling of, but can't work out how it fits into the archaeological history. The reason we are covering this information in our book is because what happened back then in Egypt is similar to what is happening now on your planet.

Egypt in the distant past was a paradise land stretching along a river. It was filled with birds and animals, and because food was so easy to grow people had a lot of time to develop their minds. They devised songs and games and were able to join together for the big seasonal celebrations of planting and harvest. They were happy.

As time passed, Egyptians invented for themselves a hierarchy and a religion, and the person they selected to be at the top to govern them would later become the only one able to speak to God on their behalves. After a time there were multiple gods and the temple priests also became hereditary positions. Taxes were imposed, and tax collectors and priests were no longer farmers or members of what was now considered the lower orders, they formed part of a separate ruling elite. It became harder to make a living from farming along the Nile and the early society stratified into labourers and owners. It continued to be an agrarian land of simple mud dwellings. This story must seem familiar to you.

What do you think the original plan was for Egypt? The first society where all people were equal or the second society stratified into layers? It depends on which type of society allows you to best learn about yourself as part of a greater whole. The first was a society of light and happiness until it became distorted. The distortion originally came from the Egyptians themselves when they introduced a variant into their game. The way they lived in the first society brought them very close to ascending in light, but they wanted to stay in the beautiful Nile valley and continue living a little longer on Earth. It seemed hard at the time for us to believe that Egyptians had forgotten the purpose of ascension and why they were on Earth. When they chose the stratified society they turned their backs on ascending.

Egyptians forgot that when they died they would return to the greater human soul and plan a new life. By living and dying they gathered experiences and brought everything they learned from life with them after their deaths, adding to the sum of knowledge and experience of humanity. Instead of incarnating in a variety of lives around the world, they chose to deliberately live life after life along the Nile. Endlessly repeating one life along the Nile did not bring enough new experiences to continue the growth of the soul. This was one of the major problems with the practice of cloning in Atlantis, the cloned souls did not learn anything new and also became less and less human with each cloning. You can tell from the excavations of Egyptian tombs that the wealthy believed they could take their Earthly possessions with them into the afterlife to continue the same life they were living here, based on their religious beliefs.

Egyptians were playing a game of discovery by creating a many-layered social structure, and they were prepared to try out new ideas. What this says about humanity is that you are curious and creative! These are human traits and need to be included in all the assessments you ever make of your fellow man. It's one reason why this particular game has swung wildly from side to side and with so little forward motion while people keep trying something new. Those who read *Planet Earth Today* will be aware of the other forms of sabotage that has afflicted your time here, but we are only talking about the nature of human beings in this book. A lot of what you are faced with today in your lives are variations of human characteristics, and when free choice is exercised it can go in an infinite number of directions, and then branch out yet again into another infinite number of directions. Predicting what is going to happen next with you can be quite difficult! Where we are accurate it is because we are already watching your future at the same time as we watch your past, each from the "now" point of view. We see the end results but not always all the steps you take to get there.

(I have watched them look for a single event in time, and they have to search through a jumbled pool of every event in existence until they find it. All events are in the pool together, not conveniently strung along a line, as everything takes place in the present. Candace)

Who are you, and how did humanity come to live on one of the most beautiful and special planets in the universe? Humanity is a glowing soul of light who lived on various planets in the past, and came to Earth to learn once again your true nature and that of your Creator. You have come so close in different locations and at different times while living on Earth, and it seems unfortunate that at times you almost reach ascension only to veer away in another direction. The decisions to elevate ruling hierarchies in the past usually led to crushing the majority of people, and gave a fine life for the few on the top. The earliest Egyptians did not know this, they didn't have a past recorded history to learn from as you do today. It couldn't be so wrong, could it, for everyone to contribute a little to the support of the ruler and the priests? This system has never yet been reversed, because the desire to change has rested with the powerless.

The early Egyptians were trying out kingship and priesthoods "just to see". Some of them enjoyed the mental activity and challenge of a whole new project. People were afraid they were missing out on something in spite of being happy in their simple lives and they developed new rules and regulations, taxes and holidays. They began to feel fortunate when they walked to the palaces and temples to watch a spectacle their money had paid for when they all joined together. Their tax money also gave to the top echelons the power to enforce the yearly tax payments. This story is not too dissimilar to that of Atlantis up to this point, but it is very different from the ascended civilisations of the Orkney Islanders and the Mayans.

The successful groups to have ascended from Earth in the past all learned to be happy, to enjoy being social and working together. The people in all these communities learned that each physical body housed a small part of the human soul, and that their neighbour was the same as they were. These societies never needed to develop cloning in an effort to cheat death. They could see themselves in the eyes of everyone around them, that all were human beings and all were the same. They loved one another and were happy. We would like to see such happiness again now as you face a changing world.

Early Egyptians were very close to reaching this point of oneness when they split into rich and poor, us and them. A whole new set of experiences were set in motion, and deep unhappiness resulted as their simple lifestyle came to an end.

7

Atlantean Expertise

THE EGYPTIANS embarked on a road familiar to us today for building kingdoms, i.e. conquest and slavery. Most people lived in mud houses, and some began to farm ever more marginal land while at the same time working longer hours for extra money to pay their taxes. Farmers were supporting the local kings, the army, the priests and administrators. The army was made up of their own sons, and the priests and nobility became hereditary castes. Slaves worked for the upper castes, not for the local farmers. You may consider this a developing society because it is more complex, but we look only to see the quality of the energy that is being emitted. There was a decreasing amount of the light of happiness.

Egypt was located near the natural land bridge leading out of Africa, and long years before the Saharan Desert grew in size there were many neighbouring peoples, some of whom passed through looking for a pleasant place to live. Egypt was fertile and attractive but was becoming less and less welcoming, while there was the beginning of a territorial mind-set. The best farmlands had already been taken, and newcomers were not encouraged to mix and stay. In our eyes this meant that the flow of energy had decreased among Egyptians. If you consider that flow is energy moving freely, and stagnancy is when energy comes to a halt, then we see this as light/flow and dark/stagnant. We angels didn't have to venture down to walk along the Nile to know what kind of changes were taking place in society there.

Egyptians became more ambitious. There were independent city-states within easy distance of the Nile to be conquered and absorbed, often today it is assumed these cities had always been Egyptian. Meanwhile, the present-day Saharan Desert was a beautiful land, green with open rivers. Many herders and hunter-gatherers lived there, and they lived with flow and light as they moved from place to place under the stars. The kingdoms along the Nile began to look threatening to the Saharans and they didn't want to live near the darkness they could sense there. Many chose to migrate further away until they felt they were out of Egypt's reach.

Similarly, people are able to sense darkness even today but it is one of those ephemeral feelings that rely on a person paying attention. When something feels wrong, dangerous or dark to you, it is best for you to avoid it. There are many examples in your world of people excusing themselves from something that later ends in tragedy. They don't always know why they refuse to take their seat on an airplane or in a boat but in many tragedies there can be a few people that avoided it all together.

You think you know about the early Egyptian kingdoms from archaeological digs, but you are only able to uncover scraps of information from those distant days. Early Egypt was one of the most blessed parts of the Earth, blessed by both climate and fertility. The people had time to do more than work all day and on into the night. They had time to consider the planet around them and they spent a great deal of the day outside. Their lives there were nothing like yours where you are living and working indoors throughout the

38

year. You burn fuel for heat and burn fuel for air conditioning. They had cooling breezes and warm sunlight, and they knew their world intimately from the clouds to the texture of the mud. They were content.

The early kings collected tax money and built ever larger palaces, filling them with precious things. We angels actually like beauty, it is an aspect of life and found throughout the natural world. Think of flowers and their scents, mountains and their rushing streams. But we do not see the point of palaces with slaves and treasuries full of gold. Eating from a golden plate is no different from eating from a palm leaf, except someone has to clean the plate afterwards, and the gold must be mined. Providing this level of luxury used up the lives of many others in service, and suddenly people stopped contemplating why they were on Earth. Instead there were priests to handle all spiritual aspects of life. People were no longer spiritual.

Being very physical and in the present can be a good thing, but not under the conditions of slavery based either on economics or captivity. Your spiritual quest is the reason you are here, and it lightens the entire energy of the physical and spiritual body. If a body has no spiritual aspect it is heavy, the heart is closed, the mind is often closed and the person makes no progress in that incarnation. This is unfortunate, as your whole purpose here is to learn about your spiritual connection to your Creator and the rest of the universe. Spirituality is like yeast and lightens the body, homogenises the energy, and allows learning and growth to take place. Once that happens the incarnation is not wasted.

You plan your incarnations to allow you to learn as much as possible about yourself. Slavery grossly limits the lessons anyone can learn by making life too hard. The effort to survive takes all of a person's focus and attention. Early Egypt quickly went from a hot-house of soul growth to stagnation where they no longer contemplated all the wonders around themselves. They could only see the furrows in front of them in the fields, or another housekeeping task; Egypt was falling back into spiritual ignorance.

Egyptians had reached this point in their development when the entire planet shook under the destruction of Atlantis. Of course it was most keenly felt by the few remaining Atlanteans who escaped in ships, but the entire Atlantic basin from the Arctic to the Antarctic was affected by the ocean's response. Who could miss the tsunamis and the water rushing to fill in an enormous gap where there used to be an archipelago? Even the Mediterranean Sea rushed out. In Alexandria they watched the water leave over the matter of a few hours. Later much of it returned, but the Sea level varied wildly over the course of the coming weeks while the Atlantic Ocean found its new level. The Earth itself, a living being, had been traumatised by the removal and the pain reverberated through the entire planet, pain that could be felt everywhere through the soles of every living being's feet.

One day a fleet of small fishing boats sailed into the mouth of the Nile. Atlantean refugees had sailed on the strength of the violent upheaval and passed all the way to the end of the Mediterranean Sea, fleeing the destruction of Atlantis. Born on an archipelago, they had marvelled at the size of the African continent as they sailed past, and they were pleased to get as far away from the site of Atlantis as they could. To the fishermen reaching the end of the Mediterranean, the Nile looked like a good place for stopping.

You are so used to seeing dry and desert land on the African and Middle Eastern edges of the Mediterranean that it may be hard to visualise the trees and birds, the animals and the general beauty and greenness of the area as it used to be. The current dryness has developed and became more pronounced over the last few millennia, but it was not always that way. The deserts were there, but they were smaller and more contained. They were filled with forms of life that found a desert the perfect habitat for their experiences, allowing them to live on a knife-edge of survival. Earth was a planet teeming with life.

Those who escaped Atlantis and landed in Egypt consisted of a few families distraught at what had taken place. Their homeland was gone, along with their beautiful white cities and the sophisticated society, but they remembered the continual human sacrifices, and the danger from the final, devastating wars.

The appearance of these Atlanteans with their advanced scientific knowledge (you have yet to catch up with Atlantean science in your world today) had the effect on Egypt that the arrival of a spaceship would have on your own. The newcomers were dismayed to see the way Egypt was structuring itself into kingdoms with rulers and slaves, but it was so primitive compared to Atlantis that they weren't worried about their own safety or their future there. These were the people who hid in the past from warring factions, and they weren't about to repeat the mistakes that made Atlantis a place of terror. The refugees settled by the coast near modern Alexandria where they fished and repaired their boats. They were welcomed by the locals when they saw the many new advantages and skills they brought with them.

At first the Egyptians were too much in awe of the newcomers to approach them and ask for instruction, but they observed them and tried to copy what they could see. The new houses were gleaming white and filled with light. How did they make them glow that way if they were built out of stone or mud? They seemed to rise out of the Earth fully formed, and they were so pleasing to look at, the shapes were organic and looked the perfect shape to fit the spot where they stood. As fishermen, they did not have to leave a lot of farmers' fields between the houses, which were a friendly distance apart surrounded by green gardens and flowers. But the gardens were never so big that they could not take care of them by themselves. These green gardens showed off the whiteness of the buildings. And *what* were those buildings made of? Translucent and white, they appeared to be made of the bones of the Earth itself. In the village centre there was often a perfectly round green space, and the houses stood around it with the front doors opening towards each other, not standing in a row. These villages were not made for horses or the traffic of carts, but for pedestrians.

How did they raise their houses up out of the Earth? Atlanteans had been taught by us to be a part of the Earth through blending their lives with her life, by knowing that they and the Earth had something in common, and that all living beings everywhere had their very origins in common in the far distant past. At that point of knowing and oneness they could tap into the power of the largest life form they were in contact with - the planet they lived on.

To raise a house up from the Earth you find the part of yourself that is the Earth. Then by sinking into the Earth and being one with her you can do many of the things the

Earth can do. She is able to erupt in volcanoes, crack open along fault lines and make it rain. These would require a high level of skill for a human to manifest. What we taught to the Atlanteans was far more useful, how to pop up a house out of the ground as an extension of the ground under their feet, how to draw heat and communication up from the crystals below. Heat was provided by the Earth and channelled upwards through the large crystals. If you were the child in a family, your parents would make sure you practiced these skills so that you could look after yourself as an adult. Just like reading, writing and cooking these were life skills that were teachable and would keep you alive. Creating an earthquake was not necessary for life, but not impossible if you were taught how to do it. In Atlantis such advanced knowledge was known and used by a very few who did not want too many to know how it was done. There is no good reason for people to bring on an earthquake or volcanic eruption, and it was used more as a threat against others. Today you use nuclear weapons in much the same way.

Understanding Atlantis is necessary for you to understand the knowledge these people had when they washed up on the shores of Egypt. Early Atlantean refugees looked a great deal like you with a few major differences. One of them was their willowy appearance and height, and another was their large domed heads. Egyptian rulers wore those high bulbous crowns for a long time that mimicked the appearance of the Atlantean cranium, and they have recovered elongated skulls from the tombs of the Pharaohs such as Tutankhamen and Ramses II. Their intellectual development was far more sophisticated than yours is today, and their routine use of telepathy developed those unused parts of the human brain.

They made extensive use of their "third eye" - the eye that senses more than physical eyes can see. One day humans may again develop craniums that look more like Atlantean ones from practicing telepathy.

After settling in Egypt, Atlanteans hoped to be part of their new country as there was no going back and they had no desire to live aloof from the local people. They also felt they could teach them about honouring the Earth and how to use her strength to make their lives more pleasant. As teachers they began to interact with the locals and show them how to raise up buildings out of the ground: by taking the molecules of stone and rearranging them to make new structures. This strand of Atlantean knowledge remained for a long time in Egypt until it, too, was forgotten. This technique was used when the time came to build the Sphinx as the centre point of a national celebration. There was much to celebrate when this structure was created, it was proof that not only houses could rise from the Earth, but also a truly large structure. The skill to raise up buildings spread among the Egyptians.

The years following the celebration around the Sphinx produced a multitude of new homes as everyone wanted to live somewhere that was comfortable, modern and beautiful. Egyptians who had already risen to a position of wealth and rulership wanted to make sure their homes were larger and more luxurious than in the past. They employed those who were becoming skilled at working with the Earth to create the palaces they desired.

As an aside, what happens when you make something like a Sphinx out of the natural stone of the Earth? The stone is part of a living planet, therefore the Sphinx is part of a living planet. There is life there, but a life that passes at the pace of stone. If you visited and waved at it, it would be a tiny flash of an event to add to the thousands of years of events it's witnessed. If you came with the purpose of talking to it, there would be an intelligent response as long as you were thoughtful and sincere. These old beings are as old as the planet, they can tap into intelligence as old as the creation of Earth itself. They are interesting witnesses to interview, and they are wise with the wisdom of the ages. Usually they ignore people, as people do not recognise that they are alive.

There is a difference between those connected to the Earth and aware of her life, and those who are not. If, like some Atlanteans, you see yourself as one with all life in the universe, including the Earth, then you often proceed to talk to everything and get a reply. Alternatively, many people do not understand their place in the tapestry of life and never try to speak with anything outside of their own species.

The Sphinx was a demonstration piece by the Atlanteans that began a new era of possibilities and prosperity for the Egyptians. This was an incredibly large edifice for a land of farmers and mud huts to possess. The Atlantean survivors designed it and raised it up out of the ground, and from that day on they were honoured as superior beings who were a level above the locals. The Egyptians believed the newcomers made the Sphinx by themselves rather than by working alongside the Earth. It is never good for anyone to have adulation directed at them, as the more a person believes they are better than others, the farther they move away from the truth. They have trouble seeing themselves the equal of the people around them. For this reason the few who have come through adulation undamaged, such as the Mahatma Ghandi or Nelson Mandela, are even more worthy of honour.

This group of Atlantean fishermen found themselves the teachers and venerated masters of the local population. They received as gifts all the best food and livestock and it became an honour if a family married into theirs. These immigrants were the earliest set of supreme rulers, married into the local ruling elite. The evils of Atlantis were not reproduced, and initially they helped the Egyptians to live more Atlantean lives. They passed on the knowledge they'd grown up with. The most damaging knowledge in Atlantis perished when it was destroyed by us.

8

Earth and Man in Partnership

IN ADDITION to raising new houses and buildings from the ground itself, the Atlantean refugees understood the relationship of the Earth to the plant life growing on her surface. If she could produce a house overnight, she could also produce a field of grain for harvest in one night. Although you cannot imagine how this could be true, plants have a close relationship with the Earth and they trust her to take care of them. If she provides the energy, they can shoot up and ripen over night. Also the Earth at that time was still awake and a fully-connected member of the universe, and she did not restrict herself to the linear time constraints of the human beings on her surface. Making a crop grow overnight is something that happens outside of time. Being outside local Earth time is where the vast majority of the universe exists. The Atlanteans felt that the most important skills they had to teach the Egyptians involved caring for the Earth and about their oneness with her. They were fully aware of the tremendous privilege of living here and loved her for her generosity. And she loved them.

The Earth deliberately provided a climate to make people's lives easy. Sun and rain were in moderation and life was pleasant; the Earth was like a mother gently caring for a newborn baby. Her main concern is the welfare of all the tiny beings on her surface. The planet delights in looking after her guests, it is the reason for her existence in this universe.

The Atlanteans began their new lives as willing teachers in this land of gentle sunshine and waving trees. The entire area was green with plant life while herds of animals wandered freely, grazing and stopping to drink at water holes. Under these conditions life was very easy for the Egyptians. Why go to the trouble of looking after the Earth? People do not see the give and take of energy that other life forms see, or realise that freely helping the planet could make their own environment and lives richer. Humanity had originally chosen not to see the ebbs and flows of energy, and the Egyptians did not always see the need for this, or feel their own connection to the planet. If you were to walk past one of your parents and deliberately ignore them, it would change your relationship with them, as your parent would feel hurt. The Earth was aware that the Atlantean civilisation had been built on a mutually respectful and fond relationship, and in the beginning life was very pleasant. Now a whole new set of people were ready to learn how to live and work with the laws of the natural world. Because the Egyptians farmed with the natural yearly flooding of the Nile, they were ready to begin learning and extending their knowledge. This mutual relationship was the norm on Earth for all the species living here except humanity.

The Nile river was a sparkling flow of water, and it carrying the energy of light through the farmlands in the centre of the country. This flowing water did away with the need for the stone circles that were built in northern Europe to unblock stagnant energy. The Atlanteans put a secondary plan into place, which was to anchor energy in the form of light directly into the planet by using pyramids. These are still one of the best ways to anchor universal energy into

48

the planet. The pyramids were planned and built in two lines along the Nile, spaced where the energy would be of most benefit. By drawing universal life force energy into the planet the farmlands were heavy with grain. Other people may have suffered from famine, but it did not happen at that time in Egypt.

These pyramids were not the funerary ones that still stand today. The first pyramids weren't even the same shape. The early pyramids were raised from the planet and were solid throughout all twelve dimensions. They acted like lightening rods, attracting universal energy to enter at the top and spread wider and wider as it flowed down into the base; from the base the same expanding flow continued down into the Earth. These pyramids were maintained by people who understood what was necessary to keep them working: pyramid technicians, later considered to be priests and priestesses. Their role was the same, that of filling the pyramids and the Earth with energy. The pyramids were like granaries, able to store light and release it into the surrounding areas to help the crops grow tall and strong.

Atlantean pyramids were far taller than the newer Egyptian ones. The Atlantean fishermen who oversaw the building of the new pyramids did their best, but they were neither pyramid architects nor technicians. From the very beginning the pyramids did not work as well as the ones that had vanished in Atlantis. A problem was that the refugees were untrained in designing a slightly different pyramid for each location, although any pyramid is better than none. Even a series of partially working structures helped, so that Egypt as a cohesive society grew in strength. These pyramids stood for many years and provided an energetic boost to the people and the land.

Similarly, in Atlantis the pyramids functioned as power stations as they poured energy into the Earth twenty-four hours a day. The Earth received the energy and it flowed away from Atlantis on planetary ley lines. Atlantis played a powerhouse role for the rest of the planet.

When Atlantis was removed from the Earth all their pyramids were destroyed and the Earth was in need of healing and universal energy. Building new pyramids scattered around the world would work just as well, as long as they were situated in the correct places and built to the correct dimensions. They were built and rebuilt for many long millennia until the knowledge was lost completely. With your new materials you could conceivably build new, lightweight pyramids (such as the Shard in London) and place them in the correct positions around the planet and they will work. Focus on the planet, follow your intuition to find the right places, and visualise what shape is needed in that spot. Ancient Egyptians, after they had fallen away from knowledge, perhaps thought that if they were buried in or under a pyramid they would be energised back into life.

How did Egyptians use the increase in light energy? This is the important question, because of the insight it sheds on the human character. Life became very easy as year after year passed with plenty of food and small crop losses. Any history of farming will tell you of the dangers to crops from poor weather and insects, and their affect on the livelihoods of the farmers. Farming could be very hard and risky work outside of Egypt. When life was very easy we could observe the way the Egyptians changed. Did they increase their levels of happiness, or did they become dissatisfied and want something more? Did they begin to come closer together and help one another, or did it drive them further apart? What we observed was the growing division between the farmers and those with armies behind them to levy taxes and rents. Life for the farmers became unhappy as they were stripped of their crops and no longer had enough to eat or sell. The ones who prospered from all this fine and high energy were the few who were ruthless enough to take and never give anything back. All that generous light of love and joy was distorted and diverted to only a few. They were the ones who lived in the fine, big houses with little work to do all day. After a while people accepted that this was how life was meant to be.

Using the energy of love and joy to create unhappiness does not really work. The energy was not used as intended and slowly withdrew. The pyramids were unusable without light entering them and they no longer had the energetic strength to remain erect and quickly deteriorated. Without the active cooperation of the Earth drawing in light and providing it for the beings on the surface, the fields of crops became less healthy and weaker. Living in paradise is a gift of the Earth, not something achieved by human actions. Using the energy of love to provide oppression only resulted in the withdrawal of the energy.

The taking of one person's goods by force is oppression, but you have all become used to that now. Some people are philanthropists and share their time and money with those who have little. But there are never enough of them to make a real difference. People who choose to act in love will align themselves with all the fine and high energy in the universe. It still exists, it is still available to you, and you may be surprised at how it manifests in your life. Abundance is a word that has come to mean money to many people today, but we do not see money as representing love. Money cannot be used to buy love.

Many years went by, the original Atlantean refugees were long dead and their knowledge began to be passed down as special secrets in a hereditary priesthood. This knowledge allowed some to prosper greatly at the expense of others, and by the time the original teachings were half-forgotten no one outside the priesthood could raise a home or pyramid. Priests held the monopoly on knowledge and wrote down their secrets inside the temples. The farmers began to slide backwards, living in mud huts if they could not afford the fees for a new home.

9

Black Magic

THE HIGH Priests of ancient Egypt used the knowledge of Atlantis to perform wonders by working with the Earth. They learned how to use alchemy, levitation, mummification and brought some animals back to life under limited circumstances. They worked on raising the human dead and hoped to achieve it one day, filling the tombs with food stores in case of this eventuality. But by that point they were no longer working within natural laws, or had any understanding of why life existed. It was a repeat of the impetus behind the cloning in Atlantis; the wealthy couldn't bear dying and giving up all their possessions, instead they wanted to live and enjoy life forever.

When the priests used levitation to raise pyramids they used working techniques taught to them by Atlanteans. Their own creative efforts were never aimed at honouring the Earth or working with her, priests were focused solely on their own prestige and becoming powerful and indispensable. By the time these priests are mentioned in the Old Testament of the Bible they are court magicians turning their wooden staves into snakes.

There are many sources of power in the universe and some are corrupt. This has given you many stories such as Faust and Dorian Gray, but they are all based on a kernel of truth. By using something that is true and building onto it with a lie you can still build something that partially works.

Turning a length of wood into a living snake is possible, but what good does it do? It is solely intended to strike fear into observers. The actions of any being will show you their heart, and these court magicians were demonstrating how they maintained their power through fear. The greatness of heart in a wizard like Merlin (his story is told in *The Downfall of Atlantis*), and the effectiveness of his actions in protecting England are far removed from these Egyptian wizards. They were practising black magic, created by themselves out of something good and pure which they twisted. Under their influence the Pharaohs, Egypt began to dwindle into a rustic society, although it remained powerful for a long time.

This is the difference between Egypt, a great nation of its time, and other countries like Britain and France that were also post-Atlantean civilisations. To take these two countries as examples, they had the white cities of Atlantis and their people knew how to serve the Earth. They did not have golden palaces or tributary states. Because both of these countries were focused on daily living instead of acquiring goods they had pleasant homes, and met regularly in their villages to channel energy into the Earth. They understood how to do this and considered it very important. In return the gardens and orchards of these lands were luscious, green and flowering with natural beauty, and heavy with fruit. They did not feel the need to create complicated lives for themselves. These people had all the food and good weather they needed and worked for themselves out of doors. There were no slaves in their societies. At this same time the cycle of bounty and famine had begun in Egypt.

Britain had in its care the great stone circles and Earth centres of Stonehenge, Glastonbury and Avebury. Because of the proximity of these and their innate functions as organs of the Earth, the people learned by living in proximity to the strong universal energy. There was a university of Earth healing at Avebury, and those who were taught there returned to their homes all over Europe and kept the weather and seasons in balance. By the days of King Arthur in Britain the trained Earth healers were powerful partners of the Earth, who could ask her to manifest help for them. The magicians of the Egyptian court could not do anything like this.

Black magic still exists today and can create a lot of damage when it is used. But its day is over and its ability to hurt others is quickly fading away as each day passes on the new Earth. This is a clean and strong planet, and black magic is a distortion and fouling of nature. It will soon become something from your past.

10

Using Natural Magic

IT SEEMED magical to the Egyptians to understand genetics as it applied to farm animals. Atlanteans no longer cloned animals for their farms once they arrived in Egypt, but during the more than one hundred thousand years of their civilisation they learned all about the breeding and genetics of animals and humans. By teaching the Egyptians all they knew about genetics they were adding to the health of their crops and animals. When this information about genetics was forgotten it was many years before it was rediscovered in the 1800s.

Animals have never forgotten their connection to the planet as they did not incarnate under the same game plan as the human species, and therefore are more content and wise in some ways. Animals are connected to the Earth and give and receive as part of their nature; there is much you could learn from all animals and insects. There used to be better balance in your mutual populations before so many animals died or were wiped out. Instead there are vast numbers of humans who are not connected at all to the planet, who have pushed the animals to the margins of existence. The necessary planet-wide balance is no longer present.

In the beginning of Atlantis we archangels were in the habit of visiting and teaching the locals about their place in the universe and why they were living on Earth. We did not need to teach them anything else, they learned metalworking and genetics through their own efforts. When they arrived in Egypt they were able to tap into the planet's strength for creation and change. How much strength and creativity is required to make a waterfall or a mountain range? This strength is available to each being on this planet, visible and invisible, but whilst you don't know how to even begin the process of making a waterfall through rearranging the landscape, the Atlanteans understood. They began to teach the relationship of the person to the planet so they would also be able to work within natural laws. They did this not to rearrange the landscape, but so that their knowledge of the oneness of man and Earth would be understood. From this knowledge everything else that they achieved was born. Much of their lives was geared to blending with a planet of love as part of their everyday living. This was the most important information they had to share, not metalworking or genetics.

The flip side of loving the planet was to do no harm to her and to return energy to her in the form of acknowledging her gifts through Earth healing circles (as written about in *Planet Earth Today*). Why was this of importance? It is important for every being to show gratitude in order to allow yourself to be given more. Gratitude is your way of receiving more through softness and appreciation. Those who have hard shells bounce any gifts back to where they came from.

What would seem magical to you? Walking across the ground and finding a hidden source of water, just by sensing it was there? Some of you can do that right now. Or knowing which direction to turn to find a parking space? Parting the Red Sea as Moses once did?

Here is exactly how to part a body of water and walk across

on dry land: first tune in to the watery part of yourself, because water is water no matter where it is located. Remember that you are one with all things, including every drop of water on Earth, and that everything is equal. Feel the presence of water outside yourself and acknowledge your oneness with it and from this position of unity you can ask the water to move aside. You are water and you choose to move aside. It is a miracle that is aligned with natural law. Water was not turned into fire or anything else completely impossible, it simply moves and remains as water. There are walls of water you've seen in surfing photographs inside of waves. Water can form walls, and it can move and flow. All magic requires practice to perform quickly, smoothly and expertly.

Magic is a word you use when you don't understand how something has happened, yet many of the mysteries you call magic have natural explanations. True magic exists in the spaces between the molecules of matter in the universe. It is present in the voids between the electrons and proton in an atom, between the molecules of the air in a passing breeze, and in the flicker of a flame. But even while you wonder about true magic, the alchemy of creating something from apparently nothing happens by knowing natural laws. A person needs to be knowledgeable and understand the substance to be worked with, such as a wave of water, then the knowledge that you are one with the entire contents of the universe (including the Creator) gives you the insight to reach out and make a change in a part of you that is external to your own body. Magic is easiest to perform with the intention to do no harm along the way. Harm can be deliberately done, and we see the damage it does to the souls of those practicing magic in that way.

An Atlantean could join with the Earth, tap into that immense power and energise seeds to grow out of the ground into plants overnight. It was possible and it did not need to be left to the Earth to decide to make them grow. When the stores of food began to run down, they would plant some more seeds. When you lost your conscious connection to Earth you lost more than you realise, more than just food. You were meant to be part of the life here, not separate or alone. Being part of the entire web of life would have brought you a different point of view and many companions. Anyone who has a pet, or who rides a horse every day knows what good companions animals can be. Living with other species connects you into the web of energy, with input from all others living here, down into the Earth and back up into yourself again. You gain, not lose by being connected to others.

The Egyptians began to create larger towns from the small villages. They still lived a great part of their day outside, helping to keep them balanced. Those who spent all day inside were the priests and the rulers. The priests set themselves to learn everything they could from the Atlanteans and ride the crest of the wave of knowledge to keep their high positions. If the people did not need them they would not have a reason to be housed and fed. Because they learned everything and wrote it all down, they were the ones who remembered the new knowledge the longest.

11

Bringing in Earth Energy

THE NATURAL wealth of Northern Africa was in its climate and farmlands at that time, and it was located at the centre of the world's civilisations in a prime position of influence. It was very pleasant to be living along the Mediterranean, the climate was benign, the fish plentiful, and it was easy to travel by land or sea. When you study your Bible and read about the small kingdoms, they are all part of this vibrant and sophisticated culture. You may picture the early biblical tribes living in the desert of today, but they lived in a healthy landscape filled with trees, water and fields. Life was meant to be pleasant, not hard work and certainly not slavery. If you are not enjoying your life, if it feels like very hard work then you are living in a modern desert, even if you are in the middle of a city.

Joy and happiness are your goals and you were made for happiness. We witness your lives today and see how worried many of you are wondering how your children will be clothed and fed and how you will be able to live. We feel that you are far off track, and the energy you produce is no longer that of joy (except the wonderful joy of children). You are currently producing waves of fear and misery. If you generate this type of energy you are contributing to a world that is made only of those emotions. You didn't come to Earth to live a miserable life; you came to be happy. By providing you with a world of fertile ease you had a reasonable start, as did all the animal life here with you.

Think of the spreading Sahara now, so vast a bird can only fly across it by landing at an oasis.. As humanity increased their own living space they decreased the land available for all other animals and insects. Worse of all are the empty oceans, the vast underwater deserts you fail to see. When there is nothing left but people, will your planet be healthy? If that should ever come to pass you will risk losing everything you came here for.

Each species of flora and fauna (including people) contribute to bringing energy through for the Earth. The shapes and songs of each life form were designed to increase the flow of energy. This is one reason why the Earth is a healthier planet when its seas are full of fish and its skies are full of birds flying and singing, energising the air and water through song and movement. Each species decided before arriving on Earth how their actions would contribute to the flow of energy on this planet. An imbalance has resulted from humanity's reducing the numbers of other species, so dulling the vitality of the Earth.

It is not uncommon for New Age adherents to practice working solely on themselves and their own problems. This will help up to a point, but for real healing you need to remember who you are and your relationship to others. Healing the planet and yourself at the same time brings wholeness with the help of a powerful ally. If you focused all your energy in healing just one of the hairs on your head you would not consider yourself a whole and healthy person. It's the same as when someone only works on their own issues. Healing needs to involve giving back as well as taking.

In Egypt they forgot how to bring in energy through

pyramids and the information was distorted and lost. The pyramids were part of an energy loop and as soon as universal energy stopped being brought in by the priests and priestesses the pyramids deteriorated. It was no good patching them up without the energy coming through to try to keep them strong. The marked decrease in the amount of energy being brought in by Egyptians at that time caused the seasons to swing more wildly with more extremes, and life became harder for the farming communities. The amount of food available for everyone began to depend on the seasons and once-a-year harvests.

This was a tangible change and it's important to see it, not as punishment, but as a lack of true understanding. Many people at that time believed the priests were taking care of the sacrifices to the Gods. They trusted that the priests knew what they were doing and that the correct amounts and qualities of sacrifices would be made in their names. The ancient world is filled with stories of sacrifices, but if you think about this even for a second you know they don't make sense. A beautiful animal is born and it will please the Gods, or appease a threatening volcano, if it is killed. What will any of these beings do with a dead animal? What did the priests do with it? (They were the only ones allowed to eat the offerings.)

12

Healing the Earth

IN ANCIENT Atlantis Earth healing circles were regularly practiced by all. An entire village would walk to a park-like area with a picnic and musical instruments weekly and set up a community Reiki healing circle. Once in the circle they would tune in and channel energy from the outer universe through the circle into the Earth. They would be eating and talking, some would dance, play musical instruments or tend a bonfire. It was a social occasion, and we thought it was a great way to bring through energy and have fun at the same time. The joy of being together strengthened the bonds of community and their pleasure contributed light in the form of happiness into the mix. It was no longer energy from the stars, it was the energy of the stars channelled through humans. The energy was transmuted and had humanity's vibrational signature on it when it was passed into the Earth. She knew it was a gift from you, and was content.

Today Earth healing circles are virtually non-existent in the West, but continue in a local form in the more "primitive" parts of the world. There are really not enough of them left now to carry humanity's signature into the Earth. If you could do one thing to help yourselves and the planet it would be to start your own Earth healing group.

Why should you? What would you get out of this that would enhance your own busy life? In the beginning the Earth made a number of contracts with all the life forms present here on the Earth. Central to these contracts was that she would provide them with all the energy they needed for life here: the energy to stay warm, to stand upright all their days and for vitality. Since the long-ago days of Atlantis you have been living on Earth and not fulfilling your side of the contract. You have chosen to live alone and disconnected from the Earth and from the universe, and have attempted to provide all your own energy through eating. If you look around you will see how that is working out in practice, as some die of famine while others have too much to eat. There used to be balance and the concept of *enough*. Having enough to live is all anyone really needs, and that includes having enough energy.

With enough energy you can live vibrantly and be warm. You will not need to eat as much and find that you heat your buildings less. There will be less need for heating oil, gas and coal. You will become balanced in your lives, and that means that the Earth will be covered with balanced, instead of unbalanced, people.

The Earth is not behaving like a balanced planet. We've said in previous writings that global warming is not solely down to burning fossil fuels, but it is down to the willingness to dig and drill as if you owned the Earth itself. The willingness to drill or frack is part of a "taking" energy, where you continually take from the Earth without return. That willingness also has an unpleasant energy signature, and it is not the type of energy that feeds the Earth with love. It exists as a blot of neglect on her surface, and she is aware of it.

All other species sing, swim or beat the ground with their hooves, sending a vibration deep below the surface. There are far, far fewer animals on Earth now. She never meant to find herself so alone and, as these species are killed off, she is deprived of the energy they create. (If you are having trouble with the concept of creating energy from your own actions, try drumming or singing and feel the change in the room as the energy lifts.) It is shocking to us to realise the oceans are more empty now than the deserts. Remember the early fishing boats that sailed to New England from Europe and met large and dense shoals of cod? A few centuries later these fishing grounds are fished out.

You are overwhelmingly the most dominant species on the planet, even if you are outnumbered by some of the tiny insect species. You go where you want and do what you will, filling almost every corner and ecosystem. If you want balance and gentle breezes from the Earth then you have to take this upon your shoulders as your own task. But very few of you remember how to rebalance the Earth. We wrote about the tilt of the Earth's axis in *Guidebook to the Future*, and how it will straighten up in the next twenty-five years or so. The Earth's imbalance extends even to the tilt of her axis, it's as if she tripped one day and didn't have the energy to straighten up. Living on a balanced world may require you to enjoy yourselves and channel some energy her way. You may also find yourself becoming warmer on cold days as you learn to connect with her.

In Atlantis the buildings and people were kept warm through crystal energy, and the huge amounts of power that were needed for dividing into male and female souls and cloning came directly from the Earth. They used very large crystals (which still exist inside the Earth) and the crystals amplified the Earth's energy. Atlanteans grew up being supported by her energy. When a living being is supported by the Earth energy rises through their legs and holds them upright. They are filled with energy and are able to stay warm because there is no lack of energy. People do not do this, instead they eat and burn wood, coal, oil and gas to keep warm. They send their energy down into her to ground themselves, instead of letting her energy rise up their legs to hold them upright. To heat an entire building or use Earth energy for the really big scientific experiments, people had to work together in groups. All of these techniques were well known. Today in order to reconnect to the Earth you must practice aligning yourselves with her energy.

We see your disconnection from the Earth as hitting the bottom of your lives here, and this is what the bottom looks like to us. From here you have the opportunity to climb back up again to the light.

13

The End of Egyptian Civilisation

EGYPT reached the bottom of their civilisation thousands of years ago as measured in the unhappiness of the Egyptian people. The great majority of Egyptians lived and worked in a caste system that supported a wealthy elite. People toiled all day and long and into the evenings, before falling exhausted into sleep. The men were frequently conscripted for months of slave labour and lived far from home while their families fended for themselves. The sophistication of the buildings and the artwork had little meaning for ninety-nine percent of the populace, other than they had provided the labour to create this wealth.

Life for most had become intolerable, living and dying as the slaves of the moneyed elite. The Pharaoh by this time owned the entire state, and allowed other great landowners to live as his tenants. The wealth flowed to his treasury, and he was considered a god on Earth. All eyes were turned towards the Pharaoh, and worshipping him by the masses was compulsory. The existence of the Creator was not forgotten completely, but was instead considered a god so remote that no one knew what to think about Him any longer. It was required to worship this Pharaoh in their midst, and obey his wishes. How could they go against their god's commands? So they toiled on, day after day.

The Atlantean heritage had now completely blended into Egyptian life, and it's origins were forgotten. The

67

priesthood controlled the lives of the people with rules and by demanding many offerings from those with little to spare. As the Egyptians became more afraid of dying and devoted their wealth to building elaborate tombs for the afterlife, they forgot their purpose in being alive. The forward movement we look for in any society had vanished, i.e. learning to love unconditionally, understanding that you are all one and that you are all a tiny fragment of the Creator. There was no focus and no energy, only the flatness of a life of repetitive ritual and a fear of death. When the reason for doing something becomes lost, it is most often replaced with ceremony and ritual.

When a civilisation reaches bottom, there is no where to go but up. In this case "up" was a return to the days when everyone had enough to eat and where each day was spent happily. This did not come about through the ancient equivalent of a destructive apocalypse, but by people simply walking away and no longer participating in their own slavery.

The people of Egypt were conscripted into armies, into work crews, and into farming large estates. Sometimes when the perfect time for sowing seeds arrived they were serving in one of these work gangs far away from their home, and the fields around the home village were neglected for a year. Starvation reduced the population of the workers and they became fewer. But to maintain a level of luxury in the top households they were not allowed to spend more time growing food. Their food was taxed in kind and taken to the cities to feed those who could pay the most for it. The farmers then did the obvious, they began hiding some of their crops so they could also have something to eat. They hid themselves when called to serve and kept their villages looking desolate and poor. Turning their backs on their great civilisation, they began to live again as farmers in simple homes, working for their own food and living under the stars. This did not happen overnight, but it all took place over one generation. Not very much time for such a large change!

Meanwhile, in the cities they were wealthy in all manner of goods and food, but they began to be short of labour in their homes and estates. They found the food to feed these slaves increasingly expensive, and the slaves were slowly slipping away back to their home villages. Villages were no longer friendly places for the government conscript squads to pick up free labour, and they were forced to begin offering something in exchange, such as land. The money in the cities had little use in the countryside and held small attraction for the farmers. By paying for what was once free labour the wealthy were forced to part with some of their property. The first steps had taken place to bring the top and bottom of society closer together.

The farmers did not feel they had much to gain, and everything to lose, by engaging with the greater economy. Once they were able to keep their crops, they felt they had sufficient possessions for a good life. They had their homes, families, fields and animals, blankets and clothing. They had time to socialize daily and talk to their friends. Their work finished at sunset and did not continue far into the night. You may think it is interesting to communicate electronically today, but the laughter and joy of a group of people is not replicated on social networking sites.

As the Egyptian economy adjusted we felt the energy change and begin to rise. From the stagnancy of flat energy, little leaps and bubbles began to happen as life returned to normal. The energy levels rose with happiness, as there is a LOT of energy in joy. And the happiness spread beyond the Nile valley to the rest of the world. There are no barriers to energy circling the globe, which is good to remember when the energy of fear is deliberately created.

The people of Egypt simply walked away from being exploited, and did not turn back. There was little drama or fighting as the ones expected to do the fighting were members of the lower populace. They stopped playing along and started a new way of living for themselves.

14

Greed Rules

YOU ARE all one soul, seperated into tiny physical bodies all busy having different life experiences. In Egypt, or any society, that has a small number of wealthy people controlling the masses, one needs to step back and look at the bigger picture. The Ancient Egyptians pushed the experiment of the wealthy elite combined with slavery to the limit of its usefulness. There was nothing else the greater human soul could learn about the extremes of wealth and slavery, and yet this pattern has been repeated over and over again through the ages with only tiny variations.

Who profited from this long series of unhappy civilisations? They increased the layer of darkness on the surface of the Earth through sadness and fear. These emotions in turn strengthened the dark angels of the universe who use these vibrations for food (see *Planet Earth Today*). A planet of darkness is the object of their game plan, and Earth has been a big success story for them. We would prefer to see you happy.

Societies with a tiny, happy elite class are usually built on either outright slavery, or wage-slavery where the wages bear no relationship to the wealth created through the workforce's labour. The overall energy of these societies is one of sadness. Within historical memory in the West, only a few of those working in ordinary jobs were paid enough to have comfortable lives. Large mansions are usually home to a single family while many work to keep them living in luxury. Because this is how it has been for centuries, it is hard to remember that life could be any different. A landowner today could take a smaller share of profits and still have enough for the biggest house in the neighbourhood and the servants needed to run it. People today are continuing to eat from golden plates while others starve.

You may think we sound like Communist angels? But we watched that system fail on the same points of greed for power and luxury as the Capitalist ones. These failures can be traced back in part to not using human imagination, to *imagining* a way of living where everyone is content to share out the Earth's bounty with greater equality. Imagine a world without greed.

A big feature of western culture is the ownership of land. Life on this planet was supposed to be free and easy; everything needed for life is provided naturally by the Earth. Yet money and ownership stand between each of us and living easily in western culture. From the moment of birth you have to pay for the food you eat, the water you drink and the ground you sleep on (or at least your parents do). Yet the person who originally decided that they owned the land did not create it, they simply declared it theirs. In effect it was stolen from the Earth and then by selling it to another human (or demanding taxes for it) it was stolen from their fellow human beings. This is a lack of love for their fellow humans and for the Earth and the rest of her non-human inhabitants. As an example, William the Conqueror created a huge imbalance when he conquered England and declared all the land to be his. This enormous act of greed is one that underlies much of western culture and is still being paid for today, not just in Great Britain, but in the cultural descendents of that time, i.e. any country of Capitalism. Because, ultimately by taking the land away from other humans and making them pay for it, you are taking away the necessities for life – food, water and shelter that come with the land. Taking and selling land results in the gifts of life being constantly striven for (this we see daily in the men and women who struggle to earn money to make ends meet). These acts of greed are the cornerstone of all the money unhappiness in western societies and are the greatest acts against fellow human beings.

Why are we ending a chapter on Egypt with writing about modern capitalism? Because we are aware of the energy emitted by overall populations. Earth reeks of sadness and hopelessness today. You have consented to economic slavery. Way back in Egypt during the first experiment of this kind you downed tools and slipped away. Today you have that option if you are willing, and it may be most effective if you shut your purses and wallets and stop spending with the global corporations. This will also help the Earth by reducing consumer waste. You can't make these changes for another person, only for your self, but it is a way of disengaging with the ones who would enslave you. Find alternatives and build new ways of living, this current way is the aberration and being happy is the norm for the greater human soul. Always remember you are a soul of light.

Part Three
How Fast Can You Remake Society?

15

The Cross Roads

ONCE YOU have reached the bottom there is nowhere to go but up. You could backtrack to where you started from, or you could head to where you've never been before. There is actually a great opportunity to create something new when building from the bottom up. Some people are perfectly happy with the way things were in the past, but if you think your life and the planet could be more healthy, then this is the time to make it happen. Think of the way each timeline ends in a new set of options. There are always new options, and you don't need to go backwards to one you've already lived through. From today, you can take any path you desire. The greater the numbers who join together on the same path, the more likely it will be the one forming your new society.

Earth's original contract with all the species here was designed to take everyone to ascension. This was an astounding plan to bring together a large number of souls

75

to ascend as one, and during the process of ascension they would blend into a single larger soul. This is a small step towards the reunion of all life in the universe, foreshadowing the end when we are drawn back together into the Creator. Humanity had contracted to join in this ascension, but was not ready. When the planet and the rest of life here ascended in September 2015 humanity was left behind on an Earth that was vastly changed. As you continue your game of learning it now takes place surrounded by ascended beings of light, who are sharing their knowledge and experiences in an effort to progress closer to God. They are waiting for you to learn enough about who you are and to join them before further physical changes take place on Earth. (This ascension was the biggest possible news story of your entire existence here on the planet, and any animal could have told you what was taking place. However, very few people were aware of it happening. This veil for humanity prevented an atmosphere of uncertainty and fear surrounding the event.) Living surrounded by a vast unified soul of light will make it easier to ascend one day yourselves.

Your lives on Earth have been entangled in a shadow web of darkness. You would take a step forward and then your attention would be yanked back to deal with something you thought you'd left behind, before you repeated the process again. Forward motion at times could often seem very difficult. Dark/light polarity is an aspect of the universal web of connection, but the dark half of the web became far too strong on Earth. In the past it played a major role in your lives here. The web of light where you simply connect to every life form in the universe is more gentle, and it seeks to support you, not control you. Its strength is in passion and love, and this is a very good combination to get things done. This web of silvery light was overwhelmed by the fear present in the dark web that governed your lives through frustration. The web of connection is central to the way the universe works, from the smallest microbe to the clusters of galaxies, everything is held in a web of energy. Smaller webs at planetary level feed into larger webs in other galaxies and the universe.

2013 was the beginning of transition between the old and new Earth following the start of the new galactic cycle (described in *And I Saw A New Earth*). Her rebirth into the new cycle includes the restoration of her balance, as she takes up her place again in the universal web of connection. Like a cog in a machine previously knocked out of alignment, Earth has clicked back into position. She is part of a tapestry made up of the families of planets and stars: or a moving 3-D tapestry. The tapestry changes as the positions of the stars move and form new associations and relationships. Stars and planets also come and go over time, altering the pattern. As she was out of alignment and not connected, how were you supposed to maintain your own sense of place? Now that the Earth is realigned once more, the sounds and energy of the universe inform her about all life in existence, and she in turn is telling them all about you. From being a planet that was not strong enough to protect the other species here, she is now a tiger. She is becoming as strong as all planets are meant to be, and her own recent ascension further increases her strength.

What about humanity? On the old Earth, civilisations were built according to prevailing conditions, but now your societies sit on top of a planet that has changed. If you were to build them again you would certainly look to take account of the energy underneath. She is a new planet whose strength is in love and light and rather than fog and darkness making it hard to find your way, she is shining outwards with light illuminating every pathway.

Many of your institutions are not made of light and maintain secrets instead that are hidden in darkness. We know that governments feel people cannot be told the truth in every instance, and that keeping you in the dark allows them to govern more effectively. Are they governing in the way you wish? Also many legal loopholes benefit only those who can afford to lobby hard to gain concessions, retaining money and power in their own hands.

Power is addictive (one of many addictive behaviours) and the powerful are filled with selfish energy. Life can feel terribly unfair to those who have lost the reins of power. The selfish will be among the last to realise that they are part of something greater; the very last are the ones who make others dance like puppets on a string for their own amusement. Because so many are unable to picture themselves in another's shoes, everyone is a rival and not a partner. They never think that the lives of others can be just as full and rewarding as their own.

To exercise power one fails to see that everyone is a brother or a sister, believing that somehow he or she has the right to tell others what to do and how to live. If the powerful recognised their connection to everyone on the planet, they would not try to control the lives of others. They would see that by joining with other humans there would be much of true value to gain for themselves. Awakening to full consciousness they would realise that they are a part of something vast and wonderful, filling their lives with love.

Back at the beginning of the universe, the Creator of us all devised various orders of angels each of us with a different role to play. Half of us were angels of light and half were the angels of darkness. There are a great many varieties of angels of light, some that are very small and nimble, and some that appear to be very large and powerful. We ourselves accept that all angels are equal, and all are part of the thought and desire of the Creator, helping Him to learn about Himself. You can read more about different types of angels and our origins in *Planet Earth Today*.

The human soul was part of the second wave of creation, proceeding from the desire of the Creator to extend His range of experiences. The history of the human soul in this universe is a long and highly respected journey towards knowledge. Unlike angels, humanity would learn about itself through a series of incarnations on different planets by devising their own living experiences and using freedom of choice. We angels also have freedom of choice, but we only wish to choose from half of the experiences available in the universe. Angels of light only choose from the light half of existence, cutting out the dark half completely. We may look as if we act under more restrictions than you do, but we can see ahead in our existence to the time the universe ends and have no wish to experiment with the dark side. There are no fallen angels, just as there are no reformed demons. To change sides would be to imply that the Creator was wrong when he asked us to perform certain tasks, which is inconceivable to us. Neither light nor dark are anything more than different ways to learn about who you are as a small part of the Creator. We believe the path of light is more pleasant, as joy is an aspect of light.

Humanity may choose from all ranges of experience, and over time has experimented with any number of games on different planets. You have taken many shapes and forms, just as here on Earth you have not always appeared in the form you are wearing now. You were once ocean dwellers and only came to live on land to experience life without the flowing of the waves. You became sluggish on land and it was easier for you to learn about yourselves when you lived in the sea. Your lives there most resembled that of dolphins. We're very fond of the playful dolphins, and we're very fond of you, too.

In the past you even lived in other galaxies. This universe is a hive of busyness, with souls coming and going from one life lived on a planet or galaxy to another. There is criss-crossing and rapid interweaving movements that form a 3D pattern, a little like a woven wicker ball. That pattern is repeated inside the galaxies, and on the surface of your own planet among the many species. By removing some species on Earth and over-breeding others you altered the pattern. It's as if your pattern or dance is taking place on a rolling boat where you are thrown together from one side to the other and back again. It's not a very balanced dance, and the boat itself is reeling and trying to stay afloat. (This is a metaphor for the alterations in the Earth's weather. She is working to balance herself now.)

In previous games humanity always sought to learn more about itself, and by thoroughly knowing itself would learn a tiny bit more about the nature of the Creator. They would get to know the part of Him with human characteristics. Humans are different from animals and insects, and these carry characteristics of Him that you do not. As you learn more and more about yourselves you may learn about additional attributes of the Creator from some of the other species. Insects are particularly cheerful, for example.

People learn from animals by living with them as they would live with another human being - with respect. Animals don't necessarily want to be your best friend but they are alive, just as aware as you are, and just as diligently living and learning. They have a soul group and incarnate here to live a life that they can learn from, and furthermore see life in all twelve dimensions. Looking through their eyes reveals a world of flowing energy and ribbons of light, all in different shades and colours. They can see the elementals that live outdoors in the 5th dimension, and who find your houses empty and stale. They also see all the angels of light and dark, and they shun the dark angels.

When a fox trots past a bush they will see the extended shape of that bush in ribbons of pink energy, or whichever colour is the opposite of the one you see with your eyes. The energy extends in a wavy pattern that most resembles the aurora borealis. The aurora borealis is a rare chance for humans to see a higher dimensional shimmer of energy (and you thought you couldn't see energy!) These small energy fields complete the appearance of plants and animals, and the physical form you see is where the energy moves the slowest. Slowly moving energy is needed to make the physical form solid in the lower three dimensions. The Earth is holding very still to give you a place to stand.

If you can't see all this energy it's because you are not using your third eye, and have forgotten how to stretch your perception in order to see the full picture. Some people are not of the mindset to see the higher dimensions. All they can see are the lower three dimensions, which is why they think planets like Mars and Venus have no resident populations. There are no uninhabited planets. Why would a planet want to be alone and not host life? That would be foreign to their whole purpose of existence.

Humanity chose a hard road when they decided not to see the upper dimensions, and it has led to a considerable amount of sadness. You've missed much of the beauty of existence, a little like having one bite of pie when you were offered a whole piece to enjoy. You also missed seeing the darkness that allows the light to be seen in contrast, and performed feats of bravery by stumbling blindly ahead. You fell into holes and climbed back out, and most of you have done your very best in every circumstance. Where you have been handicapped is by not being able to recognise those who do not do their best, and have found the rest of you easy prey. Maybe this makes you think of thieves, but the thieves we are thinking of include all these who have ever taken from you when you have no other option. That includes everyone who overcharged you in your lifetimes, prevented you from following the profession of your choice, cheated and mislead you when spending your money, etc., and especially all those who kept you from enjoying your lives. There has been too much robbing the poor from within the legal framework. Theft is theft; many of you know when you're taking money from others without justification, or when money is being extorted from you. The willingness to cheat your brother financially to have more for yourself overvalues the energy of money and corrupts fair exchange. Money needs to be enough to exchange for food and shelter, and beyond that point true wealth is not about money. It's about love.

By stealing happiness from others and by making it too hard for some to live, many have turned their backs on love. They think that self-love and the love for their immediate family will make up for the lack of love in all their actions. They incarnated to learn how to be human, but set about harming others. We've said this before in our other books: when you are all one, the second you attack another person in any way, shape or form, it's the same as attacking yourself. If you live your life this way you end up maiming your own soul and it is very hard to find the way back to wholeness.

Previously when a person who lived by exploiting others died, he found himself as part of the greater human soul. He could examine his life and find that not only did he fail to learn anything about love or humanity, he actually took backwards steps. He demonstrated so little love while alive that he had to live more lives to learn about love. Perhaps he owned a match factory in Victorian London, travelled in a carriage and lived in a beautiful home. At the same time, whole families that made the matches for him slowly starved to death on what they were paid; they could all be found lying dead in their homes, father, mother and children, and with the furniture sold long ago to buy food. The manufacturer's next lives may have been a series of impoverished ones, until he finally learned about poverty and suffering. When the old Earth ended on 2012 this way of learning through karmic lessons stopped, and the new Earth is free of karmic energy now. There is more flexibility today in the way life continues after death. There is only life, and some of it takes place on Earth in a body, and some of it afterwards as part of the greater human soul. Reincarnation is now free of karma.

So why did the twentieth century see this same pattern repeated over and over again, with a few people drawing most of the money into their bank accounts? This was a calcified pattern of behaviour, where a model set in the past continued being followed. There is one thing in common, from a Roman Emperor to a modern billionaire, and that is their lack of connection to people and the inability to put themselves in the shoes of others. Only by staying ignorant of how other people live are they able to do this. They buy their power and luxurious lifestyles with the happiness of others.

The Earth is hostess to a group of people who don't care about anything except themselves, and the rest are struggling. She travels around the solar system drenched in the energy these people emit. Or she did.

16

The End of Karma

HOW FAST can you reverse this sad scenario, and where do you imagine your human societies might go next? There is enough food and water on this planet right now for a population of seven billion to live well. Natural disasters are not going to remove vast numbers of the human population, and they sadden the survivors. Reducing the numbers of people will come via the choice to have fewer children, and by the human soul bringing people home earlier than originally intended.

Do not worry about how many people are living on the planet at the moment, as you benefit from living face to face with each other in close proximity. You may feel overwhelmed by the numbers at times, but now there is the best opportunity you've ever had to get to know your own soul group. What are your characteristics as a species, and how do you vary from one another? How far are you prepared to go to help someone else, and do you realise that helping them is the same as helping yourself? Your common soul connects into your heart and your heart reaches out to others, it is how humans connect into their own web. You do not connect through your brains. So if someone is unable to connect they would feel no compunction from accumulating as much power and wealth as possible and locking themselves behind iron gates. When you deal with these people it is best to keep in mind that they are not in your human web of heart connection, but on a shadow web and wholly unconnected to you.

This shadow web of people willing to exploit others will one day be a part of the past. The web of light and heart-connection was barely able to gain a foothold on the old Earth, and the loving links between people were limited to family and friends. Other species were not often included. This imbalance between the light and dark webs is now being rectified as a new web of heart connection is deliberately established. When it is strong and complete the web can be connected to those of other species, as well as outwards to the universal web. It's an ongoing exercise in communal effort.

Prior to December 2012 human beings lived their lives karmically, and arranged their next life so they could learn from their past. The series of incarnations where you learned karmic lessons each time you were reborn has ended. Previously, even though you couldn't remember your whole self while alive, you maintained your individuality as an individual soul when dead. When a person died and rejoined the rest of the human soul group they remembered everything they'd done in life, the good and the bad. Everyone then sat in judgement on themselves, and this is still true today. Eventually a soul was reborn and worked through karmic lessons from previous lives. As people accumulated learning experiences from one life to the next, the entire human soul learned and progressed. Karma was the method used in learning, and the absence of karma now will speed that process up.

The old Earth was a closed system where karmic law allowed humanity to learn while maintaining the blindfold. When that planet died the new Earth rejoined the universe, and a closed karmic system was no longer possible. The protective shell around the Earth burned away in early spring 2013, leaving her open to the ebbs and flows of the entire universe. Karma was abandoned as a rule for living along with the routine pre-planning of lives, and it was replaced by spontaneity. If you imagine a graph of your life, now there is nothing but a straight line ahead at a mid level. But you also have the potential to rise higher even more quickly through your actions. So industriousness and activity will take you higher and further. The opposite is also possible, where you can dip lower and more quickly through inactivity. Spontaneity is very "now" in time, it makes it hard to see ahead, and leads to the game on Earth becoming extremely volatile. Our best advice is to choose for yourself those things that you want, then go out and do them. Don't wait for them to drop in your lap, and don't drift and fail to choose. Present on Earth today are the best and strongest members of the human soul group who have earned their place by not drifting, and not waiting. These people are here to help build the future for humanity.

Some people who are alive on the new Earth chose (perhaps because of their age in this lifetime) not to join the planet on the next stage of her development, and they too will wait before incarnating again until some changes have become irreversible. The new babies being born are already connected to each other and the Earth.

The human soul resembles a soap bubble filled with people and voices. Individuals who never moved to the new Earth are not gone, even if they will not be reincarnating again immediately. First there will be some significant changes in human society that benefits the Earth. The plan is to travel

87

so far down a road of balance and fairness for both humanity and the Earth that when these people reincarnate they will not find it possible to change society back to what it is today. They will be resting on the sidelines until it is safe for them to be reincarnated. In the meantime the people who continue to reincarnate are those who have already learned the most about what it is to be a human being.

If you did not sort out your own soul group in this manner, how do you think events would develop? This co-operation within the greater human soul was planned to coincide with the new galactic cycle, and when humanity makes a decision and a plan like this it is your own doing; we are only bystanders. This is the game plan of a soul of light, and we applaud your creativity and determination to reach ascension.

Are these "resting" people evil and bad? Not really, but they were given a precious chance to incarnate and then lived lives that harmed others. They are more risky to bring back to Earth now, as their heart connection to others was too small. Instead of helping, they were the ones you needed to be protected from. These people's actions were aimed solely to benefit themselves, and they lived as if they were not part of the human race. They need to have time to learn by watching, rather than doing. If it should be that they never have a chance to reincarnate again on this planet before the human soul reaches ascension, they will still ascend as part of humanity's soul. You are all one, and you will ascend together.

In the future there will again be an Earth of exquisite beauty, with happy and healthy people enjoying their lives. The hard work will be over and you will have returned to paradise where your very bodies will vibrate with joy. Remember, joy is an aspect of light and when the people on Earth are joyful they radiate light. This is the path of ascension - love, truth, joy and light. Be happy, follow the truth and you will ascend.

This is what held you back when the rest of the life on Earth ascended. The others species had not learned a special form of chanting or ritual, they radiated light. Sad and frightened people do not, nor does a civilisation run by secrets and lies. They radiate too much darkness. When you are able to feel more love and joy in yourself the darkness in lies will feel jarring.

Will any individuals ascend ahead of the entire soul? That will be happening more and more often as many of you find the path of light to ascension leads you to become an Ascended Master or Mistress. The most common way to ascend is between incarnations because of the adjustments necessary to make your physical body ready to carry more light. From time to time it happens that someone ascends and continues in their body, but they will still have to suffer "the little death" of a moment while the body is changed to carry more light. Some of you have died longer than this on an operating table before returning to life.

What is noticeable to us is the determination many of you now have to oppose the dark actions of other men. This determination forms a strong core, and it strengthens the entire human race, allowing you to build something new and to be active. Because it's energy we're talking about it is not limited to one country or network of people, it becomes available to everyone in the world. As dark deeds are reversed the light will grow.

17

Where is the Power to Create Change?

YOU HAVE so many gifts as a species, and have wonderful brains, but few of you use them to think through arguments. You are presented with lies and told they are the truth, but no one challenges this. It would be worth your while to connect cause and effect, and think arguments through to the end. As you hunt for the truth, remember that truth is a form of light, and that by focusing on truth you will be following a path of light. You will *feel* when you diverge from the pathway, and it will feel like you've stepped down off the road you were following into a ditch. The more truth in your societies, the more light is present.

Where is your own power to create change? You have an enormous advantage over all the other beings in this universe (like angels) that never live in a physical body on a planet. Once a soul takes the risk and incarnates into a body it has the controlling say in what happens on the planet where it lives. (The risk is unhappiness while incarnate, the challenge is to do no harm and be the best person you can be. More of you meet this challenge BY FAR than fail.) Beings like angels who have an agenda (good/evil) can hope to influence a soul's actions, but are unable to take any actions themselves. Some of them spend a lot of time trying to get hold of a body to set about being good or evil in person. It hardly ever happens that a non-human incarnates in a human body, and these are usually present with the permission of the greater human soul. It is a soul of light and is mostly able to keep demons from occupying a physical body. When a demon has incarnated they are hedged around with volunteers of light to keep them from hurting people, although this is not without risk. Demons are nobody's friend.

A well known non-human was Queen Guinevere, who crossed over from her Earthly elemental kingdom to be born as human and establish a human/fairy bloodline. (Her story is in *The Downfall of Atlantis*) There have been very few beings from the elemental kingdom in the past who have chosen to be born in a human body, as they are happy as they are. However, since the 1990s there has been an increase in the number of elementals being born in human bodies. Elementals can be created by the planet at need, and are an extension of the planet in the same way as a strand of seaweed. The seaweed is not the Earth, but is a wavy extension of it in a temporary form, just as your hair is an extension of you in a temporary form. Elementals are created when a great need arises for a mobile workforce. An increased workforce of elementals recently constructed the new surface of the Earth, which she expanded to occupy, in December 2012. What's the difference between these recent elementals and the ones you were familiar with from earlier times, such as dragons and giants? There is no real difference as elementals do not see each other as "other", they see themselves as "one". They are very much on the same wavelength, with the same desire to serve the life on the planet and the planet itself. They are tied to their planet, and live and work solely with her. With her death, they also die.

Elementals who choose to be born into human bodies

today do so because they serve life, all of life, including yours. Because today humanity is the dominant species it is most effective to be born as humans. Elementals are here to add their voice in support of the planet. It is easier to avert a problem (such as burning coal in situ underground for energy, or fracking) by speaking with a human voice. Fracking has generated it's own new set of elementals working to hold together the areas being pummelled and destroyed.

The overwhelming number of beings who are non-human, but resident in a human body, are angelic. They don't have a special advantage on Earth like wings and they behave and live as humans. They may live their lives either ineffectively or as champions of light. It can be just as hard for them as for you to remember what they hoped to accomplish on Earth in their lifetime here.

An incarnate demon may be an unpleasant person, but they must be able to pass for human. By being a physical anchor point on the planet they form a steady conduit for all the demons and all their schemes, and it is much easier for demons to enter and influence events on Earth in that way. There were some present in bodies on Earth in the last century, and their main work was done by being a higher dimensional conduit or portal. It is most effective to keep incarnate demons in check through love. By being loved by other humans they may accept shackles that limit the damage they can cause in person, and help to keep their inner natures asleep.

These few incarnate demons were able to anchor darkness from the minute they were born until they died, and made it much easier for the world to become a darker place. None of them are alive now, but it is not impossible for this to happen again right up until the time humanity ascends. When the planet changed they found it very hard to continue living on her, and quickly died from natural causes. The new Earth's energy was a little like living inside an open fire for them; uncomfortable to say the least! The important thing is to see them as providing an open door, and through that door came all their brethren and all their dark intentions. If they could have disrupted a successful soul of light like humanity in their game and brought it to a dark end, then they would have won that skirmish. These people were human inter-dimensional portals for their kind. Of their many schemes we will say little here, but they were the usual type of damaging acts ranging from war and murder to control of individual human actions. Some cultures are aware that living people can be killed by higher dimensional demons, while others do not believe it is possible.

Today you are free of these human dark portals but there are many portals of light living in human form on your planet. The incarnate Elohim angels have come to collect and anchor light; there are around 1000 of them in a population of 7 billion. They are large and strong angels and go about their days as any other human. Elohim have names such as Peace, Joy and Victory, and when light anchors through them it carries the vibration of their name. Their polar opposites also exist who would anchor despair, hatred and misery but the human soul has removed them for the time being. Elohim are a collective of angels, one of the groups that exist outside the walls of the universe in close proximity to the Creator. Others are the Cherubim, Principalities, Mentalities and Seraphim. These angels exist inside and outside of the universe at the same time, and all have kept a small presence on Earth over the years.

You are on a new planet filled with light, with many resident angels and humans who anchor light. There is every chance for this light to expand and fill your societies. Once the energy of love and light is widespread there are those who will find it a little too uncomfortable to continue living on an ascended planet. Here is one difference between humanity and interlopers: you are the soul group who is meant to be here. You signed a contract giving you the right of residence, and these others didn't. If there is a problem here like the current imbalance of weather on the Earth then the best help for her is the human race. There are far more of you present here than anyone else and you are strong. No one can make you follow their advice or guidance, and no one can save you if you choose to go down. The greater human soul from the start chose to ascend with the planet if it could.

18

Using Death to Change a Planet

REMAKING society fast can sound a bit frightening, so let's break it down. First we're suggesting that as love increases it will start shaking the foundations of everything you have lived with in the past. In a world of love, any change will eventually be aligned with love. Even the people who do not seem to act in a loving way may alter their behaviour completely. Right now, you would be happy to see any new signs here on Earth that helped you live without fear or worry.

The people born during these last few decades were the best ones who could help at this time, and others stood aside and ushered them forward to take a place. Those who chose to step onto the new Earth are the strongest and most balanced human beings, they have the job of tearing down everything that no longer serves love and light, and build something new. These are the individual souls who will choose to reincarnate over and over again until the old society is gone and a new one is on the right track.

In this way death becomes a tool to remake the Earth. Death is the other half of life, and is just as powerful a way to create major change. As death gradually removes those who are not present on the new Earth, people remaining to work on planetary restructuring will find that they have less and less opposition. These people are not perfect, but they are connected through their hearts and will work to make a world based on love, where everyone is treated as they would like to be treated themselves. This is the most important rule that applies here. When you treat others as you wish to be treated yourself, you will have grasped that you are all one.

As the years go by change will come about because of the people alive now. They will refuse to go along with the final actions of those in their last incarnations. The people leaving to rest are as human as you are, and you still need to treat them as you would treat yourself. But you don't need to do as they say. When damage is being proposed that only benefits a small minority, those are not people connected by love. Instead they are people to be resisted. Remember, strength no longer lies with them.

Did you ever wonder why the human life span on Earth is so short? Human lives are very short compared to beings living on other planets. Short lives were your fail-safe clause in the original human contract for living on Earth, added because of the blindfold you were wearing. If one of you turned to evil, your personal ability to cause damage would be limited by your short life. This was another reason why cloning in Atlantis was so detrimental. By remaining incarnate for 20,000 years as one soul in a succession of bodies you circumvented your own fail-safe arrangement. Atlanteans went too far in the wrong direction because of science and cloning.

Today you are so afraid to die that you maintain your hold on life for as long as you can. There is only life, part of it in a body and part of it without - physical life or spiritual life. It is a gift for you to die and leave behind a worn out body, returning to your spirit life. It was designed by the human soul as the way you would learn on this planet, and for many long ages of your life here you crossed over with ease, surrounded by family and friends. The fear that surrounds death and what happens to you after you die did not exist. You were as wise as any animal and left your bodies behind when rejoining your soul group.

Today there are those in nursing homes with only the smallest connection to their bodies, their souls look a bit like balloons anchored to the physical body by a ribbon When you think someone with dementia is "not present" it's true that very little of them is there. They have almost gone beyond the point where they can consciously release themselves and will have to wait for their bodies to stop living. In the meantime, they are souls holding light for humanity, and when the need for this recedes then dementia will also be less common.

It is good to remember that some people incarnate to live shorter lives. They finish their plans on time and are ready to leave, even children can finish what they came to accomplish and be ready return to the human soul.

Death was once so visible as a part of everyday life that it was accepted with ease. Death surrounded you as you lived closer to the other animals, and with your elderly living in your midst. Now only those with pets or in the food industry may see an animal die, and old people are dying out of sight in care homes and hospitals. It has become distasteful and something to avoid being in contact with. As a result, only a tiny number of people now have seen one of the larger species die. You see dead birds and insects, but not the animals who look at you with big sentient eyes. Birds and insects have sentient eyes, but they are so small and quick that you don't register what you are seeing in them. Even your pets now are put down by veterinarians instead of dying naturally. They have not forgotten how to die, and could teach you about death.

When you are faced with the death of a loved one, it would help *you* if you thanked them for everything they have taught you. Be happy they are embarking on their next phase of life returning to the greater human soul.

19

Three Changes to Make a New Future

L IGHT is rising from the Earth today and shining
through everything, even if some people in governments
or business choose to ignore it. It will be noticed that they
are out of step with what the majority of people want and
that you are voting at the ballot box or with your wallets. It's
slowly happening.

When you look around and see bad things being done
by your fellow man, these are people who put up cast-iron
shields against love and do not connect through their hearts.
They do not receive love through any cracks in their armour
and few will respond with love to you. Now that the ascended
Earth is building her levels of light we can see these people
as dark spots on her surface. To be a person of darkness
living on a planet of light is to live inside a fire. Their life
force will burn ever more quickly and they will be gone. They
have shortened their own lives.

All you have to do to change your society is to go with
the flow of energy, following your instincts about which
actions to take. When the governments and businesses begin
to follow and deliver what you want it will be in response to
aligning yourself with the new energy, and it will be a relief.
If you are reading this book you are ready to change more
quickly than they are.

There are a few ways to make change happen and a big

one is where you shop and bank. Your money keeps many large corporations going at the expense of local businesses. There was a phase when large companies joined together, until now there are only a few to choose from and they all seem to be the same. Do these companies serve you well? Maybe some do, but they become focused inwards and it becomes all about their own income and growth. They may talk about their customers, but customers are outsiders and don't belong in the inner circle. Even shareholders who own the large companies are often excluded from the full profits, as corporate salaries rises higher and higher. Within large corporations prices are manipulated and your buying choices become limited, while keeping costs low, often meaning that the principles of fair trade are ignored.

Social change happens by viewing others with love and accepting that your family is as large as the entire human race. If your child's house was destroyed by high winds you would rush to help her find shelter. All of these people in disaster areas are your brothers and sisters, and when you show that you love them and want their well-being to be equal to yours, you have changed and your society has begun to change. Rather than envisage exact equality, imagine a world where the rich are less rich, and the poor are better off. The top and the bottom of society draw closer together financially instead of growing ever farther apart. There are going to be any number of opportunities to help others in the years ahead. This can range from lobbying governments for borders to be opened to refugees, to sending them food or money. Think of a world where you help the ones nearest to you, safe in the knowledge that others are doing the same for those nearest to them. Instead of tragedy there is the opportunity to show love, and then there is simply more love in the world to be shared.

When there is more love everywhere there is a softening of energy, and it's easier to remember that you are a splinter of one soul. Instead of fearing what is coming next, where the fear spreads igniting more fear, you have changed fear to love, and dark to light. Take as an example the lives of the people in northern Nigeria who are living in a war zone of rebellion. They don't know if they will be attacked by rebel or government forces, and their livelihoods have been ruined. Constant fear of each new event is all they have in life as their children die from malnutrition. Nothing to do with you? You may be buying the gas or petrol to run your cars from Nigeria, the fifth largest producer of oil in the world, thereby supporting a corrupt government that fails its people.

Political change can come about through becoming involved with your local government more easily than through the national level of the political parties. The experience you gain from working with local people and getting to know them, will lead you to either form a new political party or to change the present parties from the inside. The current political parties could serve more of you better, but at the moment they are wobbling in their imbalance. When they get to the point where they no longer have the public's support they will still be in power unless you have made an effort to create something new. Politicians control the purse strings and assign government contracts. It's a hugely lucrative business, and is interwoven with the large corporations that receive the contracts.

There are governments that threaten the lives of their

citizens as in Syria today. You may feel that any government that deliberately harms its citizens will be the last to change. These are the countries that could yet surprise you, as they may contain fewer barriers to realising you are all one. Perhaps the change to loving your neighbour will begin there? Once change begins it can't be stifled inside a single border but will spread beyond, especially when it is a change that is good for people.

It may sound so simplistic that it can't be true, but the energy behind love is so strong and noticeable to every non-human on the planet that it can change the immediate environment. A couple of thousand years ago people flocked to hear Jesus speak. Jesus was filled with love and it rippled out from him in waves. People wanted to be close enough to feel that love, they didn't see the love. Love is warm and fuzzy, and feels good to be around. It also spreads very quickly. (Warm and fuzzy? Which type of person would you describe as cold and hard?)

Three main changes are needed to remake society: love, spending money locally, and political changes. You can change fastest by releasing everything that keeps you from loving your fellow humans and all life on the planet, including the planet itself. Withdraw your spending money from outsiders and you can make your area lively by supporting local businesses. Local economies could be reinvigorated within a year if you joined together. Politics is the slowest to change, but the way you govern yourselves will be closer to serving your needs if you start with local input, and build up to a new way of living together. A community established on mutual respect and love will not support a hierarchy that is out of sync with it.

20

How Change is Working

THE ENERGY at the top of society underpins its hold on power and possessions, never allowing anything to slip away to someone else. The rigidity and tension of holding on so hard are part of the current energetic picture on Earth. This could be illustrated by the tip of a pyramid that is almost rock-hard with the tension of gripping onto possessions.

Below this top, there is fluidity in the middle with a rising and falling of wave-like movements. The middle is more about holding a variety of ideas, and the acceptance that others may be right. Through acceptance of other viewpoints creativity rises and risks are taken, allowing change to happen more easily. Possessions do not mesmerize their owners so tightly in the middle. Pink transformational energy swirls through this area, horizontally. The middle is the healthiest, on a strictly energetic level.

The lowest level of the pyramid is stratified into thin layers, and the energy that mixes here does so in layers no thicker than a pancake. This lack of vertical mixing has resulted in rigidity and stagnancy in the thin layers. The feeling of "us" inside these encompasses very small groups, and movement between them is almost non-existent. Too much energy goes into maintaining strict boundaries against outsiders.

Take the whole pyramid and apply the energy of change to the bottom and it will start to simmer and boil as the bubbles rise through the lowest levels and begins to mix them. Bubbles then rise into the middle level where they pick up speed and continue mixing. The increased energy will cause the bottom layers to vibrate, shaking the rock-hard top as they rise through the middle layer. Imagine a rigid pyramid top set onto a vibrating pile of jelly, in the end that top will slide off to one side and crash. There is nothing harder than trying to hold onto your possessions with bleeding fingers in a maelstrom of change. Change is stronger than anything else in the universe; no one is strong enough to hold on in the face of the whirlwind of change.

Change happens at the perfect time and the perfect speed. What happens after you see those first simmering bubbles in a pan of boiling water? As long as heat is applied the process continues with the bubbles coming ever larger and more quickly. Your role in all of this is to let it rise through you and release any obstacles you hold to change.

21

Assistance from the Earth

WHAT DO you want to change? This is down to your own wishes and creativity. Humanity has been on Earth so long now that you have lived many different lives and experienced many different forms of society. You do not have to keep repeating the ones you have already lived through. You who live in the West may have lived in simpler cultures in a previous life. People from primitive cultures may have already lived in the West, and may not need to do so again. There is an ingrained judgement against living in truly primitive societies where people are considered less good and inferior and in need of Western help. These cultures are not inferior, they are simply different, and they offer a different experience to your own life. Because all these various societies exist on Earth right now, you can be sure that the next developments for humanity will be different once again. You outgrow your societies quickly as you learn the lessons inherent in the current ones.

When you found yourself on the new Earth it was because you chose to work towards the end result of human and planetary ascension. You were the strongest individuals, and many of you have allowed your light to shine as best as you were able throughout the years up to December 2012. In some lifetimes this was hard to do, as you went against the accepted habits of your societies, and those who incarnated into the most unforgiving cultures were the strongest souls. Any who held open a door allowing a crack of light to shine through onto the Earth, even where the local theocracy was the least tolerant, were the ones who were the strongest . Maybe some of these people don't appear to have accomplished a great deal in their lives, but they kept their countries from drowning in darkness. Once a country has lost all its light you are on the road to recreating Atlantis, and you have no need to repeat that experience. People are teaching and working as they did before, but now they have the wind blowing at their backs pushing them forwards. Let's consider a healer in a country that has no regard for healing; people were helped by her but many did not want to talk about their good experience because they were afraid of what others would say. This healer doesn't need to change what she is doing, but the energy will help others to recommend her. She is offering what everyone is looking for.

How exactly can you make this happen in your own lives? You need to persevere and not give up, and you need to believe in your own success. The Earth has changed now, and by believing in your own success you weed out the futures that are unsuccessful. You have to participate in creating your own lives, and need to dismiss thoughts of failure. What you worry about is what you end up creating for yourself, and why would you want that? You create a future path that includes success at what you do, along with happiness, fulfilment and love. That's your half of the work needed to succeed.

The new Earth plays her part by matching your efforts, by providing a clean and wholesome surface to live on. She is like a little star radiating light in the higher dimensions, and that light supports everything based on love, and destroys plans based on the lack of love. This is what allows your own plans to come to fruition, and surrounds you with people who support you. For the first time you will be living in an environment that helps you by matching your energy and easing your path onwards. The combination of your efforts and the benign surface of the planet will lift you up. If all of you who are light workers are lifted up, as if on ladders, you can see each other and make contact. By working together and supporting each other you add to your personal happiness and success. Individual change can happen as fast as you are able to create it.

This is the beginning of a new epoch on Earth. Everything you have learned and done in the past has brought you to where you are today. You are the right people in the right place to take action and change the way you live with the Earth. Your original plan for this galactic cycle was to finish the old ways of doing things and start something new and more delightful, and you are being deluged with quality assistance to realise this plan. The actions you take will be your own, and they will come from your heart.

It's all going to happen much more quickly than you could ever imagine.

Part Four
Trouble Along the Way

22

What Slows You Down

A NGELS write books to try to influence you and help you change. We can't make you change; only you are able to do that. Our desire is to help you enjoy your lives on Earth, because that's not what we see now when we look at humanity as a whole. Readers of our earlier books leaped enthusiastically with both feet onto the new Earth, eager to take their lives further. Our books had worked to decrease their fear, and whetted readers excitement about the world of the future. The new societies on Earth would not be based on ideology or business, but be based on happiness. If you think happiness is out of your reach, look at all the other free-living species on the planet and observe their contentment. You have created a way of living that is constrained and stressful, where people trudge through their lives filled with worries about the future. If this doesn't describe you, then you're fortunate. There are so very many people on the planet who struggle to make ends meet.

The Earth is now an ascended being of light, and humanity has a wonderful opportunity to learn about themselves surrounded by the vibration of love. There are a lot of people alive on Earth who did not choose to move forward with her when she was reborn in 2012. Many never even noticed that a change was coming, or had any understanding of what was about to take place. In contrast, almost every life form: plant, animal, insect, crystal and more, were excited and ready for the change. Many people were aware of the chance to live on the new Earth and yet still chose not to come, and some who had begun to move forward changed their minds and remained behind through complacency or fear. Those who chose not to come did so within the personality and lifestyle they have in this incarnation.

There are people (and all Earthly governments and businesses are currently filled with many of these people) who are in their positions because of the decisions they made and the actions they took on the old Earth. Very few members of religions or cults are living on the new Earth, as they could not contemplate anything other than what they had been told by their leaders. And yet, even these people could see that the world was changing beneath them and they had a choice whether to stay or go. They were afraid of what they did not understand and did not trust their own intuition. It is important to respect everyone's personal choice, if you look down on others you are simply despising a part of yourself. Many of these individuals are going to continue living as they did before, and act as they have always acted. Those who did not come to the new Earth are the people with potential to delay the rest of you. Their souls connection to their body is thinning and stretching as the new Earth accelerates away from the spot in time where the old planet vanished. It's important that you don't think of the new planet moving away in space from the location where the old planet used to be. This isn't about up, down, in or out; it's about the dimension of time.

The complex issue of time comes into play when we talk about the old and new Earths. There have been many old Earths, and only one final new Earth - the one now in existence. The old Earths existed in galactic cycles of 26,000 years, as they were born and died as regular as clockwork. You have variable and unknown life spans, but the Earth does not. Hers are timed by her journey around the galactic centre of the Milky Way. There are many planet Earths that existed in the past, and are no longer part of your present. Every day that passes takes you further away in time from the old Earth. Humanity blindfolded itself to universal time in order to learn about how life is lived in linear time, as the lessons it teaches are different. We wrote a great deal about the changeover from the old Earth to the new in our book *And I Saw A New Earth*, and it is a story of great hope for all in this universe.

When we say that this is the final Earth as you have known it, it is because she has now ascended in this cycle, and continues to learn new lessons at a higher level. You originally planned to ascend with her, but when the day came humanity was not ready.

In April 2012 each and every one of you living on the planet was offered a choice of whether or not to go forward onto the new Earth and continue your lives there. About forty-five percent of the global population chose to go forward at that time, mostly younger people and those whose hearts were already connected to others and the planet. By December 2012 some people had reversed their decision, for the most part because they were afraid. Few knew what going ahead with the new Earth might mean to them. Many of those going forward were people who enjoyed being outdoors and they believed the new Earth would be an even better place to live and took the chance. And now today, what is different? How is this Earth anything more than a continuation of the same?

It's been a few years now since the Earth's rebirth on December 20, 2012. Ever since that day there has been a shift in the underlying energy, with all change taking place below the surface. It's been a time for removing the old and replacing it with the new solely on an energetic level. Every change begins in the energetic layers around an object, being or situation. As the changes take place at the point where the energy has the highest vibration and is furthest away, each change feeds down through increasingly dense layers to the very centre. The outer layers are easier to alter because they are more energetic and fluid, and align more closely to the energy of light. If you think of two people who bump into each other, they each have a small effect on the other's solid body. The effect is far greater following a change of heart. The energy works into the heart and broadcasts outwards on the new frequency, and helps to change others by altering the surrounding energy. Two energy fields bumping into each other is therefore not an accurate description of what happens, as each field temporarily blends into the other. During the moments they are united subtle information exchanges will take place. This is part of the process that takes place when assessing the health of another person or animal when together in the same room.

The key to learning about other species on Earth is this blending of energy fields and exchange of knowledge. You have assumed that you learn by using your senses and your brains and building on experience. That does happen, but it doesn't explain the person with intuitive knowledge. There are gardeners with green fingers, horse whisperers and other experts, and they bring an enhanced level of understanding to their work. When you wish to hire someone who is really good at their job it is often for their ability to navigate away from making mistakes. Understanding plants or animals by blending with their energy bodies and absorbing what you have learned there, allows you to see the shift in their energy fields before they reach the point of action. For instance, if a horse is going to buck and rear, first the energy changes, then they roll their eyes and kick. By reading the change in energy the expert is ready to act.

2013 saw the start of changes in many human societies around the planet, and there have been physical changes towards creating balance in the planet itself. In life, first you choose a direction and then the road appears beneath your feet. You are not used to thinking of it in this manner, where you create a path by your own choices and actions. You feel that every path through a forest has already been trodden by many feet. But we are talking about your own path through life. Have you ever met anyone whose life exactly duplicates your own? It's impossible, even if you have a twin there will always be some variation. Establishing the energy first, and following it with physical action is how you create your own path. This is why it is so important not to drift along aimlessly in life. Life will still happen every day, but without direction. Drifters live by responding to other people's choices.

Would that be such a bad way to live, and aren't you meant to go with the flow of energy? We want to be clear about the difference. Drifting aimlessly is taking a turn on the surface of the Earth and learning life's lessons by accident. You have had many, many opportunities for your soul to learn by accident and it brings little new information back to the greater human soul. Often these people learn nothing new to add to the sum total of human knowledge at all. When too many people are drifting it greatly slows the speed of change, like a river of slow-moving molasses. This way of learning is no longer useful.

If there is one aspect to life on Earth we hope to teach you, it's that life here is a learning experience, and when there is nothing more to learn from a particular situation it will end. That is why as a species you move from one way of living to another, without the need to repeat a previous civilisation. Whenever there is a step backwards in a society it can feel very wrong and is usually short-lived.

When you are between lives you are busy choosing your next learning experience. No one plans to drift aimlessly, but instead arrives with a plan for life in mind. Once a human is born the plan is forgotten, but the birth parents form a starting point for the baby's life and are part of the existing plan. If it is "I want to be a musician", then there are music lessons, after-school practices and joining in with others. The energetic choice is made and the path grows wider with every practice session. If that person one day says they want to do something different they make a new road while the old one fades away. It won't be there for someone else to walk on, everyone needs to make their own way.

We are talking about how you create paths because it is time to focus and walk on some new pathways. When a society ceases to work for everyone, then a new pathway may be created that leads away in another direction. Without the existence of karma your choices could lead you somewhere new very quickly, and on a new Earth there is less baggage to hold you back. For example, we're not saying to walk away and refuse to pay your taxes, but perhaps to earn less, own less, and pay correspondingly fewer taxes. Instead of being told how to live, choose how to live, and when you're tired of that choice, pick something new.

23

Who's Living on Earth Now?

IN SOME ways it has become much harder for you since 2012, because the Earth is filled with people who are physically present while their souls are on the old Earth. As time passes the connection between their bodies and their souls is stretching ever more thinly. The human soul had planned for this fresh start and originally thought 80% or so of the population would elect to continue on the new Earth.

Currently the people with increasing distance between their bodies and souls tend to be those holding positions of wealth and power they were unwilling to give up, and there are still many on Earth who unknowingly support them with their own energy. These people do not understand what has taken place in the last few years, and they continue to live the same lives they always have. Do you understand why we say it would have been most beneficial if 100% of the population had chosen to come onto the new Earth? At that figure there would have been no one opposing plans to help you balance the Earth. Instead you have 35% of humanity living here with body and souls together on the planet, and 65% who do not. There is a stronger opposition to change than anyone ever thought there would be on the new Earth, and that's what makes it harder for all of you. It is also difficult that in the industrial countries of Europe, Asia and the USA the percentage of those who came forward onto the new Earth is the smallest. Your world leaders are drawn from these wealthiest countries and are those who have no real presence here.

This is a difficult concept to understand: the fact that some of you are living on Earth, and there are other people living with you (perhaps even in your own home) and they are somehow present and not present at the same time. We do not feel it is clear enough to say "they're not here," and need to explain it. To begin with, up until April 2012 you were all here living your lives and the plants and animals were looking forward to the rebirth of the Earth. Their attention was fixed on the centre of the galaxy, and they were waiting for the burst of light that brings change. Some people were also aware that change was coming but very, very few understood what it would mean. Many people subconsciously began to prepare their own lives, to be ready when the time came. We wrote about the wave of energy that would carry people as if they were on a roller coaster on a wild ride into the future. (In Spring 2012 the archangels were writing a number of channelled blogs about these changes on www.candacecaddick.com.) In time the wave of energy arrived and many people climbed straight onto the waiting roller coaster. Others had no idea there was a wave of light arriving, but when they sensed it's arrival they also climbed up and took a seat. Family members began to look up and see the coming wave and perhaps their children or parents sitting ready to leave and because they loved them they also joined. Still others looked up, saw it and said "I'm too busy", and let it leave without them. Some people joined the ride into the future and at the last minute climbed off and remained behind. The wave of light carried its passengers from the old planet to the new, depositing them standing on their own two feet. Looking back they saw the chasm they had crossed, and they saw people turning away from the edge and walking back into the old world. It is one of the stories of your soul group, what happened at the time of the wave and the birth of the new Earth. One day humanity will tell it to many listeners who want to know what happened on Earth at the beginning of her final incarnation.

Those who did not join the wave, or changed their minds before the end, did this for many personal reasons, but one of the most common was exhaustion. Some human souls have had many, many incarnations, and for some this current life in a century of war and social divide was lived under great stress. No one was required to go or to stay, and many of those who chose not to go were older and ready to rest. This is why we said that this life formed the choices of those who went and those who stayed. It's so important not to judge anyone who declined to come, as you won't know the reason why. You can only make a blind guess. Those who did go forward were ready to continue their work for a balanced Earth.

Others who live among you are here by the grace of the Earth. She has many small life forms living on her surface to care for, and she understands that the best way to keep everyone alive is by being as stable as possible. We know that those that are really here are full of interest and expectation to see what happens next, while humanity is oblivious to it all. People need to be supported with energy, and just as an animal will draw up Earth energy through its four legs, so people will need to learn to draw energy up into their bodies. Because the not-present people can no longer do this, they must be plugged into another power source. That source is the people who support them either ideologically or through the family. No one has to be a power source for anyone else, we find it repugnant unless it's done through love. The term "psychic vampire" covers behaviour of this type, and your fictional zombies are not too dissimilar to bodies without souls. It's no accident zombie stories are currently very popular.

Change will take place in spite of human efforts to prevent it, as we wrote in Part Three. The young people of today will become leaders in their turn, and they will begin to make a difference. They will never become the same type of person their fathers were, but right now the young are being slowed down and delayed through society's indifference and overall opposition. There is currently a lot of forward energy, but many of the new leaders are unexpectedly missing from your ranks after they missed their chance to mount the wave, and that has left you with too few to take full advantage of the new forward energy. Some of those who are missing were people who incarnated specifically to help in this period of change, but failed to arrive on the new planet. Why? Partly because it was too difficult to educate everyone about the reality of your world whilst being bombarded with misdirection and lies. To take a new and balanced planet forward each of you here will have to step up and make a difference.

Those of you who came on the wave of light are the ones who were ready to help Earth to be as lovely and healthy as possible, and also become balanced themselves. They wanted to be happy and fulfilled and were not the type to shut themselves away and count their money. You are part of a group of diverse, talented, aware and alive people who aren't afraid to speak up. It's just that everyone (including the greater human soul) thought there would be more of you. You have the ability to hear and sense when you are being told something that is not true, or not in your best interest. The words of not-present people contain very little energy.

What if you don't know if you're on Earth or not?. Or don't know if your family is here with you? Turn your focus on your own body. You should have a sense of presence, of energy, and of being here. You can detect roundness and a 3-D shape. Next look at a tree, they are fat with energy. Look at something made of metal or wood, like the background on a TV program such as the News. Which has more energy, the news desk or the presenter? Does the presenter look flat, or perhaps even like a dip or hollow in the energy? Focus on the Earth, and try seeing if the person carries the same energy as the Earth. If you can see the aurora borealis, you can see this! Watching TV or live performances are a good way to practice - keep on practicing until you can see the different levels of energy. When you can tell who is on Earth through sight and sound, you are ready to walk forward without being distracted by people that aren't fully present. There will also be a few people whose energy is quite different. These may be incarnate elementals, angels or other beings.

If you feel your family may not have arrived with you, then you may choose to support them with your love. Be aware that they may make some decisions that no longer make sense to you in the new circumstances. You will need to use your new way of seeing to guide them along the straight line you are walking. It won't always be as easy as if they had jumped with you, but it does mean they will continue to share your life. Filling your life with people who love you and whom you love is what living is all about.

One thing that will not happen is that people will suddenly all die at once. The greater human soul is taking action, and some people will not have enough life force to remain on Earth as long as they'd planned. There are many whose life spans have been shortened as a consequence of their inability to see others as one with themselves. They no longer contribute to the growth of the soul, and have become part of the problem that hindered humanity's own ascension. Some voluntarily left earlier when they realised that they're not part of the new world. They are the people who saw they'd missed their chance and slipped away easily by letting go of life. The great soul that is humanity is home to all your souls, please think of every death on Earth as someone going home, not as a punishment! They will be home, and continue life in their spiritual form. When all of the people from the old Earth have died, the remaining population will consist of those who were either born after December 2012, or chose to come in April of that year. The balance will shift over the years as births replace deaths. There are children on the new Earth under ten years old who did not choose to come, just as there are people over ninety who did. Some countries had very, very few come over, while others had almost the whole population.

24

Breakdown of Society

THE MOST calcified social patterns today are in the West. When something is calcified it can stand alone by itself, like a stalactite. Calcified patterns can extend from long-standing chaos and violence in Africa, to the banks and stock markets of Wall Street. Wherever there is a status quo to be upheld and fixed patterns of behaviour there is calcification and atrophy. Imagine people standing inside a stone tower that rises ever higher above the rest of humanity. If there was no tower and all these people were standing on the ground there would be freedom of movement and a level playing field for all. At that point, huge changes would take place in society. No one would have a job simply because of who their parents were, and all would now have the same opportunities. And here is where making your own path really comes into its own. A level playing field full of unique people will walk without hindrance into the life they desire. And it will be easy.

Calcification of society relies on everyone continuing to live exactly the same way as they always have. It's about believing there are proper ways to do things or anarchy will result. You have been living in a period of anarchy on your planet, beginning approximately 2500 years ago. It's time now to dismantle stubborn and harmful patterns, not by attacking them, but by refusing to play along. For example, banks make a lot of money from customers. If you don't like banks, stop being one of their customers, and put your investments and savings in alternative places. If there are no alternatives today, stop and think about where and how you would like to handle your money. By thinking "it would suit me to put my savings ...." you have begun something new right then. How do you think some of the eco funds in the stock market began? Someone wanted them to be there so that they could invest in them. Actually, quite a few people wanted them to exist.

Today some people with spare money are joining together to keep local shops and amenities open. That way they can keep a post office, shop, pub, etc. open through local ownership, sharing the administration and profiting by living in a town that's alive. You don't have to be the one to create every new idea, but you need to stop and think about what you want. Stopping and thinking, serious planning and, above all, meditation can create many new ideas. Follow the ideas that appeal to you, and let others follow the ideas that appeal to them.

One of the problems for you right now is the height of these calcified towers. Because they are so very tall and already filled with people, entrance can seem beyond your reach and you feel daunted. It's all very well to talk about level playing fields, but how do you change the status quo? This is where you can learn to use healing energy to affect situations by changing the energy surrounding the established way of doing things. Softening the energy around a calcified tower will weaken it and help it dissolve. Energy is softened with gentleness and love.

Some useful ways to dissolve hardened energy include using Reiki healing in a group or even by yourself. Reiki is healing energy, and will help to soften rigid energy patterns. Or one could visualise a gentle rain dissolving the structures. That is exactly how change can come about, by even one person holding a healing intention. This would also be very suitable for a group visualisation, or to do within a meditation. For instance, holding a situation in mind such as the lack of opportunities for women in high level government positions, the effect of Reiki would be to dissolve barriers. This can manifest in any number of ways over time. It is often something that is easier to notice when looking backwards at the changes taking place over a couple of years. Ignoring existing structures and moving ahead with your lives will weaken them and stop them from becoming stronger.

There has been an increase in the number of adult children of MPs running for Parliament in the UK. That will make it harder for an unknown person to be selected for a seat and reduces the vitality of the institution. All of these institutions lose vitality when they become exclusive and hard to enter. They are missing out on all the new ideas and talents that outsiders might bring with them. When you are faced with any profession that only takes on new people through the recommendation of those already there and by selecting people who are "one of us", they're already well down the path to stagnancy and darkness.

In theatre the third and fourth generations of acting dynasties are now performing in films and on stage. At the same time there are more and more informal fringe festivals showcasing new ways of entertaining audiences. There is a broad base of entertainment that is fresh and new, and delights people just as much as the traditional theatre. Just ask someone who's taken part in an interactive theatre experience if they've been having fun.

Crystallized patterns, rigid viewpoints, inflexibility, and returning to the past are all hangovers from the old Earth. It may seem very difficult to dissolve all of these, and we admit it will be a little harder because so many people are reluctant to move forward. Because these attributes are of the old Earth they have no future at all and will not last, as they ultimately have no planetary support. It is going to be very different for you when you realise that the being who really carries weight and has the final say is the planet. The Earth's support is required for every aspect of life on her surface, and that includes the way humanity lives. The Earth is providing the light now, and that means all will change. It affects whether you live with love for your fellow man, or whether you can hurt another without your conscience troubling you. It also means that an established institution can crumble as fast as anything else on this planet.

Light is energy, as you know, and it rolls across the universe in different wavelengths and colours. We often say that once the energy changes it will manifest as something new in your life physically. You are living on top of a planet in a state of change, and change is also coming towards you from the stars in the form of light. Light from below and light from above has the spark to initiate change on Earth without your help, so how can this go wrong? Isn't light stronger than humanity? Do you have to do anything at all to make change happen or do you simply keep living as you have always lived?

One possible problem for humanity is accepting that we do not own the Earth. She invited us to her home, and we came here as guests. Once here we began to lock up some of the other guests, kill, maim and poison others, and make the surface uninhabitable for a great many species. It wasn't our planet to ruin. If you had a party and some of your guests began killing the others you know how you would feel.

Who are these other guests that humanity is harming? They are the polar bears, rhinos, bees and many more species who are either dead or vanishing. They were innocent victims, invited here by Earth to experience life.

The Earth notices when humanity digs below her surface, but she's big and it's only surface damage. When we kill off her little ones - the plants, sea life, animals and insects - she becomes fed up with people. It's as if you were invited into the playground and started killing the other children. How dare humanity do this?

You need to visualise human ascension in order to make it happen, thereby creating the pathway and the energy first. We angels are guiding you to building the thoughts leading to positive activity and to bring about ascension. It's about choosing to move forward in love and not becoming paralysed in fear because you think it's too late. It's not too late, but you have to take steps to live with love for all Earth's children. You are living surrounded by light now on Earth and have all the help of the higher vibrations of an ascended world. There are fewer obstacles and more help for you to ascend than at any previous time on Earth. Everyone is cheering you on as you finish your difficult game.

You have a choice in front of you: to join with the rest of life and take your place in the universal dance, or to stand aloof. Each is a possibility, and each leads to a different result for your soul. No one is going to make your choices for you.

25

Eyes Shut Tight

IT'S IMPORTANT to realise that in spite of the good will and positive help coming your way, you can still refuse to change. The entire universe can change around you and yet you can continue to stand alone just as you do today. The world can transform under your feet and you do not have to transform with her. So what on Earth is going on?

One of the wonderful Narnia books by C S Lewis is *The Last Battle*, where those who are fully conscious and awake watch the world change, and as the old Narnia falls away they rush "further up and further in". The new world is in appearance just like the old, but it is more alive, the colours are clearer and the air sparkles. If a hand is laid on a tree they can feel the life quivering inside the trunk. It is the same world, but healed of all its hurts and just as it was always meant to be.

At the same time as this rebirth is happening in Narnia, the black dwarfs are sitting in a donkey's stable refusing to see what is taking place. They remain behind and congratulate themselves on how clever they've been not to be fooled like everyone else. The others give up on them and go on ahead into a planet filled with life, while the world of the dwarfs shrinks to a filthy donkey's stable. *The Last Battle* was written over sixty years ago and shows you life on Earth today as some choose to go with the changes and others do not. Some will enjoy the world as it was meant to be, while others will live in ignorance of it never seeing the beauty surrounding them. They remain alive but their lives are circumscribed by their refusal to see.

Let's take another example, the movie *Pleasantville* made in 1998 begins in black and white but as the story progresses the film changes into colour. More opportunities for happiness are created and lives become many-layered. There are problems to be resolved before everyone moves over to accepting that the new world has expanded into colour. It is an apt metaphor for what you will be experiencing over the next few decades until the changes are complete and everyone is living in the same world again. We often use modern media to tell our point of view and help people understand our words through day-to-day examples. Once we archangels sat on a rock and taught those who gathered around us, now we help inspire creative people to tell stories to a very wide audience. If you learn something that makes you think from a story or movie, enjoy playing with the new ideas. Life is for learning and living.

There have been many books and movies over the last few years that include snippets of universal truth. They show you a picture or give you a single idea to take you further. Movies and TV were the first to show you a black US President, and made it easier to accept an elected black politician when the time came. The first man to cast a black actor in the role of President took a risk, not knowing if the audience would accept him. The risk decreased with every movie and TV show made featuring a black actor, and by the time a real election took place much of the risk had been eroded. This is how we often work today, if you pay close attention you may be one of the first to hear our messages for yourself.

26

The Path to Your Future

THE DAYS are gone when you could take an action and it carried little weight or significance. Each of your actions lays down a paving stone before your feet for you to step onto, and your next action provides the next stepping stone. The phrase "following your path" is still used, even in this book, but it is not an accurate representation of what is happening now on Earth. Your individual actions construct the path and they will take you wherever you choose. One option could be for the path to curl around you in circles, so you keep taking a step in every direction but never make much forward progress. Another option would be to focus on a goal and brush everything else aside. This would hurry you along in one direction, but you may have brushed something valuable out of your life. We would recommend creating a path that gives you a pleasant journey to your goal. The purpose of any spiritual pathway is not arriving at your final destination, it is the journey you make. Each of you will create a unique pathway for your life, and therein lies an obstacle. Humans can find it hard at times to work together towards a goal.

The original plan for an incarnation is often to learn something new, or to reinforce a lesson learned in a previous life. Perhaps that lesson was as simple as learning how to say "no". Quite honestly, that's an enormous lesson that involves self-esteem, life management skills, and perhaps a few crises as friends, family or an employer become upset. But the person who understands their own value can one day learn to say no, even if it takes more than one lifetime.

It's important also to understand that life is not about striving, and that life happens every single day simply because you are present on Earth. We have said that it's important for you not to drift directionless through life, and that life is lived by creating a path before your feet. We want you to actively choose the life you desire and that makes you happy, adding to the sum total of happiness on Earth.

You were born with an objective in mind and with lessons to be learned, and when you planned your life they were your inner guiding desires. Although there are many ways to learn more about yourselves, if you are inactive it limits your progress. Ideas set your direction, and your actions take you along. For some people this is very obvious, while others may spend a lot of time mentally creating a direction without ever stepping onto the pathway. Another group worries about being on the right path, or did they make the right decisions and are they travelling at the right speed? The answer to all those questions is yes, as there are no wrong paths, no wrong decisions and no wrong speeds. You will not end your days without having learned anything new or without being ready for a new life and new lessons.

We mentioned that life is not about *striving*, and you can either travel in a relaxed manner, or by being stressed with worry. Worry is self-fulfilling; the more you dwell on something you don't want the more likely it is to happen, and the negative energy of worry creates the pathway you walk on. It may take years, but you are creating exactly what you don't WANT. To dissolve your negative projections you need to cancel, cancel, cancel every thought that projects a bad outcome. You can focus Reiki or light on all your previous existing negative thoughts and let the light dissolve them, and you can build up the trust that you will always be looked after. Therefore it's important to cancel thoughts, dissolve old ones with Reiki or another method of healing with light, and trust that you will always be cared for.

Another way of creating what you don't want in life is to be unkind, and to treat others in a way you would not wish to be treated yourself. By living in this way you have turned around and walked back to where you started, as if you have learned nothing about being human. So what? This kind of person has become pointless in their existence, and is irrelevant as far as learning anything new to add to the sum total of human knowledge. But they are also living in a way that sets an example for others to copy. Unkindness spreads, and it is part of the lack of love and the blindness to reality that covers more and more of human life. After a while it seems to be the normal behaviour entrenched in society, leading to people disconnecting from one another. Another person's hardships seem to have nothing to do with them, as if they did not all share a common soul. In the end the journey to understanding becomes a longer and slower road for everyone.

Every now and then a person completes their life plan when they still have years or decades left to live. That's when we get to watch the inborn creativity of humanity, at the point when someone can choose any life they like. Often they choose something new that they never experienced before and are able to get a little head start on another incarnation. Not even their next incarnation, because in timelessness it is irrelevant to string lifetimes together in a line. Think of a pool of incarnations, and one of them will now have a little jump-start of knowledge. We are not trying to bombard you with difficult ideas about time, but Earth-time has come to an end and the veil of time is ready now to be removed. If anything in one of our books starts a little rip in the veil of time for you, that will help you to one day remove it completely.

There have been many opportunities to incarnate on Earth and continue learning during your long residence here. You have been searching for the knowledge of who and what you are, and by learning as much as you can about yourself you will learn more about the One who created you. The universe was designed to help the Creator learn about Himself by having as many different experiences as possible. He made beings seen and unseen, and the human soul contains a very creative part of His spirit. Not every being has the same qualities: consider the dog on Earth. This animal holds a part of the Creator that includes unconditional love and loyalty in far greater quantities than exist in humanity. Dogs learn about themselves when they live with love for humans or with loyalty to the pack.

There have been many shifts in balance between the half of the universe formed to express love and light, and the half that encompasses fear and darkness. In the very beginning it was half and half, and as the games on planets began the darkness and light strove against each other to be the only energy present. In a universe of polarised dark and light opposing each other, they still have the same function: they each teach the Creator about Himself. The lessons they bring to Him are of equal value, and they are often completely different. Something as dark as a war can provide the setting for the brilliant light of an act of selfless bravery. They work together, while working against each other. We are the angels of light, and our other halves are the angels of darkness (explained more fully in *Planet Earth Today*.) Their appearance may be scary and unpleasant, but it helps them do their job.

What we angels of light have going for us in our opinion, is existing in bliss and beauty. Planets that advanced through learning games all the way to the light are joyous places without fear. The games played today on these planets teach all about happiness. The dark angels have different methods of motivating people and the most common and effective one is fear. If you look at those who generate fear in others you will see how readily they are obeyed, and fear leads to unhappiness. We try to coax you into being happy, and they threaten you with fearful consequences. In the end you reach either total happiness or total misery and have finished that particular game. If you finish in light you may then choose to move to another planet and try a new way of learning.

On Earth you have been heading rapidly towards a game ending in fear and today you have far more fear here than anyone ever dreamed you would have. To change this, each one of you can create a little pocket of personal happiness and allow it to touch other people's lives. You changed your own life, and in this way you can help change someone else's. Each of you who finds a happy way to live removes a bit of energy from the dark half of the balance sheet to the light half. The only way to change the world is to change yourself, and if enough of you do so you will align to walk in the same direction. A number of people walking in alignment is the most effective way to speed up change on the Earth today.

Seven billion people travelling on their unique pathways are still one soul. As an example, if one group of people works to make as much money as they can by exploiting tar sands for oil, they are walking in one direction. If another group wishes to stop them and shut down their industry they are walking in the opposite direction. The human soul arrives at a stalemate, like a wagon with two horses pulling in opposite directions. It's time now for humanity to make forward progress, to bring together enough people on one pathway to start moving in the same direction.

What would happen if this wagon raced off in one direction only, perhaps because there was a law passed to stop all activity harmful to the Earth? Think how fast that wagon could go now! Because there are still a lot of old Earth people living here, the weight of numbers is on their side in the short term. Those of you who came to the new Earth by choice will need to be active and vocal in her support.

27

Working to Bring About Change

THE HUMAN soul has been living on Earth for a very long time now, and you have learned approximately 98% of the lessons you came here to learn before the end. The remaining 2% is not so much about learning new lessons, as about remembering and reliving those that are not quite embedded firmly enough. If you stop and look at the world around you right now, can you guess how this game will end? Will it be in happiness or misery? We are putting this question to you because it is your question to answer, not ours, and your actions are the only ones that matter in your game.

This part of the book is called "Trouble Along the Way" and that makes it sound like you have a chance of ultimate failure in your soul's mission. You will not fail, because you either take the lessons learned through happiness to the Creator, or the lessons learned through misery. Failure is not possible. But you may have already decided that you want to take the pathway of joy. To do this you will have to make sure you take the actions that lead to personal happiness. While you are busy doing this, you may notice that there are many who are not taking any actions at all. They may be counting on someone else to act. If we put it in the context of learning: the person who works out what their next step is and then bravely follows through will learn the most. The Earth's population appears to be made up of some people who are moving under their own steam, and others who are being sucked along behind them. What does this mean for humanity and the Earth?

If there are enough people with sufficient strength to choose happiness and walk straight towards it while not allowing anything to divert them, then they will begin to pull others along behind. If you have ever done this in a swimming pool you will know that it does not involve additional work to have others flowing along behind you. The water does the work of sucking them along. It may seem a little unfair that some people are making their own way and others are along for the ride, until you remember that you are one soul and you all share the same outcome. We come back to the point made in previous books that your very best people are here on Earth right now to help the entire soul ascend. You are working on the planet with the support of everyone else above who is not incarnate at this time. The higher selves of even the least helpful humans on Earth also support your actions, but their incarnate selves are having trouble hearing their own higher voices. Humanity will not be very happy if it falls into darkness on its final game.

To make real progress it will take a sizeable number of people walking on the same path at the same time. Gathering people who feel the same way as you do about life can widen a pathway first into a road and then into a highway when working together. A highway allows more traffic to flow in the same direction more quickly, and that volume is what will build the changes toward the light. For example, if you want to eat organically grown food you can learn from others how to grow it for yourself, or you could teach others, or you could join together to sponsor a farmer to grow food for you by guaranteeing to buy from him. With the final suggestion, a path is established wide enough for others to see it and imitate you by following in your footsteps. They are being pulled along behind you and their participation accelerates the pace of change.

Maybe you've tried forging a new path and no one seemed at all interested in joining you. When did you try? Was it before the rebirth of the Earth? Because now you are going to have to trust us that things have changed. Not for everyone, but for all those who are actually present on the planet now. They are here because they can see the light with their own eyes and it is so beautiful that they only want to walk towards it. They are ready to learn about anything new they can do to bring this light firmly into their own lives. If you have something to teach about living in harmony with the planet, healing yourself and others, or about building a fairer world, now is the time to speak up and be heard. Those with the energy to act are here with you, and the old world people will become less and less effective. They are like ghosts whose hands are unable to grasp and hold objects.

We want to be very clear about the way forward; it happens as you talk with others who agree with you and you all align your actions in same direction. Joining together to travel in one direction will come naturally to you, especially as the veils you wrap around yourself begin to tear and dissolve.

Angels are aware that in the Western countries, individualism is highly prized and working together can seem less desirable. The entertainments you watch frequently have the "lone wolf" or "rogue" policeman as the hero, and the establishment is corrupt and foolish. You accept this as truth, but this is both too simple and too complicated to be true. Let's start with humanity as one soul, imagine all seven billion of you as one body where some of you are fingers and others are organs or skin. Humanity will work best if you all work together to support the whole. When you have a cancer tumour or rheumatoid arthritis part of the body is striking out on its own path and harming the rest, as a simple example of how individualism can harm the whole.

But what about the corrupt establishment that needs an honest person to be the whistle-blower and put a stop to what is happening? This is more complicated and is only successful when you support the whistle-blower, and then it stops being only an individual who is acting. There is often going to be an individual or small group who begins the process, but they need people to support them. The more people who stand together the bigger and stronger is the wedge driven into the corruption.

What if the American people had stood behind Edward Snowden? His whistle-blowing had world-wide repercussions, and his revelations of surveillance were accepted to be true. People around the world benefited from his actions, and even in the US changes were made in routine surveillance of the population because of Snowden. But he is still a man in exile, wanted and vilified by the US authorities. He began making the wedge that could be driven into the heart of corruption in many security services. The wedge could be larger and more effective today if citizens would allow themselves to be pulled behind him. Look for yourself at the after-effects of whistle-blowing and come to your own conclusions. Too often people only listen to the voice of the establishment.

When is the establishment the good guy? You can tell by how it feels, and you feel through your heart. To do this you need to stop thinking in your head about what you are hearing and let your focus drop to your heart where your soul is anchored. Your soul is not easy to fool and it will pick up the vibration of either fine and high light, or low and threatening darkness. You may have never consciously tried this before but you have all done this subconsciously. It is often referred to as a gut reaction, or feeling rather than thinking. Sometimes the brain simply cannot think its way through a problem, but your heart will always know. You will feel doubt when you are being lied to and rather than dismiss this follow it up to explore the inconsistency between what you feel and what you hear. From feeling that something's not right, you can go back into your brain and figure out what may be wrong. Easy examples of this are all those business communications that start with "to make it better for our customers...", and when you look at their changes you can see it is only for their own benefit.

The section "Trouble Along the Way" was included in this book so you would all understand there is no room for complacency. You are being gifted with all the help the beings of light in this universe can provide. But we cannot act for you, we can only advise. As much as we want you to ascend and live in bliss, having new experiences at a higher vibration of light, we can't make that happen. The learning challenge on Earth was yours, and you rise or fall by your own actions. If you end up choosing misery then this is the final game for humanity in this universe, and it will end only when the universe itself ends. Darkness includes stagnancy and lack of movement, and stagnating on a planet that slowly deteriorates will be the conclusion. As angels we urge you to allow yourselves to move forward as individuals, then as small groups, and on into ever larger associations. You are natural movers and used to flowing, it is unnatural for you to remain still. The only reason you do not move forward is because you are afraid. Don't ever be afraid, it will be easy once you start following your hearts.

Part Five
Starting Over With Light and Fairness

28

Early Years of Restructuring

IN PART FOUR we wrote about people joining together in groups, creating broader pathways, and developing so much momentum that humanity can't help but travel in new directions. The objective will be to establish a society that treats others with love and respect, leading to ascension and blending with other souls here. You may read about climate change and worry about the future of life on Earth. You have not yet finished your time here and there are even more paths to create, choosing the next direction is completely open to you. If you choose a pathway to correct the effects of poverty or global warming, then you may need to create it with your own two feet.

On the Earth there are many good people. They do not want a ruined planet, or poverty-stricken lives for others living here. Instead they feel they would like to help and take actions in their own lives to slow down climate change or alleviate poverty. But they don't know what is best to do. It may be hard for you to imagine an entire planet of people

following your lead, but it could happen exactly like that!
You may set the example in your own life by helping others
and enjoying the experience, or you could start a petition
to curb a harmful development. Just the fact that you are
changing from passive to active, sets that energy moving and
flowing. It will tug at others to act, generating interest in
new ways of doing things.

Each step you take can be in any direction you desire.
Your path on Earth is solely determined by you and is not
pre-determined by other people's footsteps. It's time for
many of you to turn around and start walking in a different
direction from the mainstream, thereby showing others
a new direction for humanity. You are able to personally
walk away from global warming by changing your actions.
The Earth may continue warming but you will always be
in the right place at the right time, with all that that implies
financially and domestically. Currently the actions that lead
to climate change are filled with greed, but acting with love
for the planet and other species carries the opposite energy
and has the opposite effect. Again, first the energy changes
followed by changes in the physical world.

There is already a core group of you who work hard for
the Earth and who worry about the health of the planet.
You know you are not alone when you see an international
organisation like Greenpeace leading a protest against
damaging practices. They are active in the industrialised
countries, but are actually a very small organisation in the
larger picture. What Greenpeace does very well is to remind
everyone that there are serious problems to be addressed.

So who else is part of the core group helping the Earth?
There are many, many people who are silent but who support

living with the Earth in a mutually beneficial partnership. These range from small-holders and allotment gardeners in the UK to Amazonian tribesmen to city gardeners in New York. That last group is looking to get their hands dirty and be in touch with the magic of growing plants. Many people now live with pets and learn about love through their companionship. There are billions of people who live and work away from cities and close to the Earth. This is your largest group that relates to the Earth daily. These people do not know how to go about joining together at the moment, but they have learned the difference between the light of truth and the darkness of lies by living in closer contact with the planet. When some of you begin to say "no" and walk in another direction, these are the people who will gradually turn and follow you.

That will still leave on Earth large numbers of people who do not see the need to work together for humanity, the next generation, the planet or anything else. But as we pointed out they will not be alive forever, and the balance will slowly shift as people are born and die over the next couple of decades. Humanity has also put a severe restriction onto itself: if an incarnate soul was not able to work for the good of the whole soul group then it will have to give up its future incarnations on Earth until it learns better. Those who already learned this lesson will reincarnate here over and over again in the years to come, with very little time in-between lives. Those who stepped over onto the new Earth in this lifetime have no need for time-consuming lessons between their incarnations.

Each of you is aware on an inner level of the overarching human soul that divided itself into physical bodies in order to experience life on Earth. Subconsciously you always knew who you were, a shining soul of light and love filled with ingenuity and creativity. At this moment in time, those of you who are true to yourselves come the closest to living the life you planned when you incarnated. Your physical self clicks into alignment with your soul's purpose and you finally become whole. So many of you currently appear to have your soul's purpose out of alignment with your body, unbalancing your entire presence. William Shakespeare said it perfectly when he wrote "To thine own self be true".

One attribute the human Ascended Masters and Mistresses all share is that while alive they completely integrated their outer actions with their inner soul's purpose. Humanity as a whole wishes to ascend to the next level and join the Earth, and people will need to become aligned, as the Masters did. All creatures on this planet are on a quest to express their souls through their lives and actions.

There are those who destroy the happiness and lives of others by starting wars, theft, murder and destroying the planet. Their actions make it possible for you to learn to survive through kindness, resilience, and co-operation, as New Yorkers did following the destruction of the Twin Towers on 9/11. The Earth has changed, and you've changed with her. Never in the past were you able to say that all who were born after a certain date are truly different - these are the children with stars in their eyes. The balance will tip towards the light as the years go by with births and deaths, until all those who profited by hurting others will have died. If their children also did not choose to come to the new Earth, they will become outnumbered by those who did. They may even learn to care for the Earth and others during their lifetimes.

This is why we said a new way of living with the planet will one day be firmly enough established so that there will be no going back.

A number of new souls will be incarnating with specific roles to play on Earth, those who will help gather others together into groups by using the web of connection. These new souls will carry such a great amount of love that they will draw others close to them, and instead of people feeling separated they will recognise their common humanity.

The new souls will be created from the combined experiences of all human beings. For the first time they will include a little piece of many individual souls, creating beings of great love. This is a way humanity has devised for itself to progress, to end the current stagnancy and to try a new approach. The rules you play by on Earth were created by you, and you have the scope to alter them yourselves. Useful gems of experience will be gifted to create these new souls.

In the past there were great masters who incarnated one by one to teach about love. These new incarnations will be men and women who teach about love by example, by who they defend, and by what they resist. Humanity has a habit of forming a new religion around each of your great teaching masters. By sending so many to Earth at once we angels and Ascended Masters hope to avoid this, and these souls will begin to change everyone they come into contact with.

29

Indigo Children

WAVES OF new types of souls have incarnated on Earth in the past. You were blessed with the Indigo Children over twenty years ago. These young people are hybrids, great beings of the universe given permission to incarnate in human bodies. They are important on Earth as those who see clearly and recognise truth from lies. They do not like the unclean touch of lies and point them out to others. They are lightening rods who attract attention to themselves, and the discussions that follow can open people's eyes to the truth. Their purpose is to help everyone by exposing inconsistencies and often corrupt motivations. They are all over the world and will have the most influence with people in their own age group.

Indigo Children are here to help the planet and all life on Earth. They incarnated as human beings because right now you are the dominate, planet-changing species with the greatest power to help or harm. The Children arrived over a short period to create a ripple of change and demonstrate another way to live. Indigo Children are establishing themselves now in many spheres of life around the world and they will be the ones who find a new way to either sidestep or resolve old problems. Don't be afraid to take advice from a young person; they could be offering you great insight and hope!

Originating in the stars, Indigos are human while living

on Earth and at the same time are ancient and wise beings of love and service. They are so old that they have visited many planets over time to instigate change. When their physical body dies they will return to their soul group and resume their normal way of being. As individual fragments of an ascended soul they know they have nothing to lose when they incarnate in a human body for a lifetime, and the changes they create here are rippling out past the confines of the Earth to every part of the universe. There is no time delay on the universal movement of energy, it does not need those tick-tocks of Earth time to limit its speed. Indigo Children are also learning and extending their knowledge while helping to change humanity.

At this time they are present in the arts, as teachers, athletes, tour guides and anywhere else they are in contact with people. They do not work in dark corners or industries harmful to the Earth. One finds them mixing with people and making eye contact. They inspire others to be the best they can be, and are very creative. Some are familiar faces from your media coverage. A consensus develops around their ideas and they create movement and flow, and whatever their colour of skin or religion they live outside the boxes others try to shut them in.

Indigo Children sacrificed their own pleasant lives of love and joy to live on Earth and help. Love and joy are the gold and diamonds of the universe, where the end of every quest is to find love and happiness, and sacrifice can be a way to achieve them. The universe is blessed to have this great soul of service as part of its family of light.

30

The Peacekeepers

THE NEXT wave of souls coming to Earth are the Peacekeepers, and the colour of their soul will be white. (Human souls appear red energetically.) It is now time for the whiteness of truth and light, and they will embody this like a white flame. Their births are beginning now and the majority of them will be born before 2020. These new souls will have the role of restoring peace to troubled nations and troubled souls. They will not condone violence, and their influence will flow across the world like oil on troubled waters. They will finally bring about peace, and at that moment all of humanity will breathe a huge sigh of relief at the end of organised murder and the resulting grief. A soul that is killing itself brings pain far beyond the confines of Earth. It is a vibration of misery that can be felt throughout your galaxy, its echo travels far beyond. We angels are drawn to your planet by the cries of grieving mothers and wives and children, and we remain here to help.

The Peacekeepers are your own solution to humanity's problems. Imagine the greater human soul collecting knowledge learned through many individual lives. It's similar to each of your body's cells reporting back to the brain. Your brain does its best to sort out any problems by trying to find a solution, and this is mirrored in the action of the human soul. In addition, your soul group is conscious and whole, wise beyond anything you can imagine right now. This soul has chosen to allow incarnations for Indigo Children and Peacekeepers.

In the past there were incarnate souls who carried love so strongly that others crowded around them. The story of Jesus is well known; people wanted to be near him to feel the love he carried. He showed you the wholeness of love, the sustaining energy of it that keeps you alive. You, too, could choose to live in that light and feel like that always and follow his example, or the example of another great teacher such as the Buddha.

For a long time we hoped many of you would find love so fulfilling that you would chose to live that way every minute of your lives. We angels live like that, but we are not wearing blindfolds and so are able to see all of reality. After reviewing past errors, the human soul is going to demonstrate how serious it is about the its failure to ascend. Humanity has a new plan - to incarnate a number of people simultaneously, separately from the Peacekeepers, who will show love to the world as a necessary condition of life, and who will replicate that part of the teachings of Jesus and other masters. Imagine a few people living this way in every country around the world simultaneously. They can't all be the founders of a religion, or so special that no one else can ever be as good as they are, can they? Humanity is a soul of love and light, and by incarnating people who live by showing others so much love that people flock to them, it will change the social environment. Being greedy can be a role model for some, why not copy those who are kind and loving?

For this to work, kindness and love will need to be valued for their own sakes, and to carry as much importance as a bank balance carries now. These new souls will be born into your world, and they will need to be protected from harm while growing up. The Peacekeepers will work to change society so these new Masters are accepted and helped. When they begin to set an example, your populations will need to respect and support them.

31

School for Souls

IN THE PAST, following the death of a physical body
the soul rested and eventually returned to Earth to take
up a new body and life. Now only those of you who chose
the new Earth in 2012 will be present and work for her,
undergoing rapid-fire reincarnations. This will continue until
the ascension of humanity. The light that was central to the
new planet matches the love inside these people. Those who
did not choose to come along onto the new Earth at that
time will be entering a "school for souls" to watch and learn
from the results of their actions whilst alive. It will take a
number of human lifetimes for some of them to understand
that when they had their chance on Earth they chose not to
care for others or the planet, but instead worked solely to
increase their own power or wealth.

All the knowledge and experience needed for humanity to
ascend is present now in the human soul, but it needs to be
put into use. Life isn't about understanding what needs to
be done and then hoping someone else will act, it's about
using the knowledge in a positive way. People on Earth in
the future will live happily by making the Earth healthy and
whole once more. They will see that the veils are thinning
between Earthly illusion and reality, and they will use their
knowledge wisely for the common good. Cleaning and
healing the Earth will eventually heal the entire human soul,
thus bringing closer the time of ascension. By the end Earth

will look like Narnia from the CS Lewis books, where all the species live and work together as members of a world community.

The early years of restructuring will include a backlash against those who act only for themselves. People who are actually present body and soul on the new Earth will find that they have the energy and power to be effective in their actions, and when they oppose new and harmful plans they will succeed. It is necessary to build momentum and early public success will inspire others to take action. Small wedges will be driven into the heart of problems in many countries simultaneously.

Sometimes it can seem as if there is so much opposition to change on Earth that success is impossible, but that is no longer true. We write this to encourage you to act now and not wait. The underlying change you were waiting for has already happened, and it's your turn to create a pathway of light.

32

Oceans of Sorrow

DURING the coming years, the Earth will work to rebalance herself. She will start by enhancing the habitats for many of her smaller creatures. So many areas now are reduced in variety and quality, and the ability to support life is debased in many environments. The oceans empty of life are one of the best examples. They were once filled with living creatures and plants, but now are so over-fished that people eat smaller fish from smaller catches. The changes go all the way down to the depths as sea populations crash. Humanity has not behaved sensibly with regards to the harvesting of fish and other sea creatures. People are eating for today, as if empty oceans won't matter for future generations; at the current rate fish will become an expensive luxury. Do you love the Earth and her oceans enough to change this, and what do you think will happen if you do not?

The Earth depends on her seas and if the oceans die by over-fishing and pollution, the planet herself will die. If the water in your physical body was fouled and did not support life you would also die. This goes beyond the deaths of sea creatures, it encompasses the stagnation that occurs when there is no remaining life to swim and stir the depths. Oceans need more than the wind on its surface to keep the energy moving. There are very few places remaining with sufficient life to keep all the oceans alive.

By abusing the oceans you have introduced a note of worry into everyday life. There are relatively few individuals who decided to pollute the oceans, but everyone has to live with the consequences. The oceans are not something separate, but form a setting for your life on dry land. They are like a beautiful, fluid picture frame surrounding a painting of your lives on dry land, and all of you were aware (at some level) that spoiling them diminishes your own lives. Humanity is not separate from the rest of life on Earth and deep down you know this, it is the truth at the heart of your existence. A healthy ocean carries the energy of life itself. It teems with fish, with movement and with happiness. To strip it of life striped it of happiness. The two-thirds of the Earth's surface that is ocean has become sombre and sad, and this is the energy that flows around you now instead of happiness. The energy of the world you inhabit is important.

Imagine you were living on a world covered in joyful oceans. The energy of joy would be enormous, large enough to be felt far from the water itself. Water would carry this energy and you would find it in rivers, in rain and in the kitchen sink. Liquid joy. Instead it is a flow of sadness and you live with it because you have no choice. The emotional energy of water may be a new idea, we encourage you to tune into it and feel it for yourself. Then start to do something about it.

The oceans today are seeking balance, and one way to reach balance is to have a more flexible arrangement with dry land. The oceans are becoming more than a picture frame, they are becoming part of the picture themselves. Islands and continents used to come to a firm end at the water's edge. Land is adjusting to sometimes being covered with water, and sometimes being dry. People will need to leave for high ground when water encroaches, and move back in the dry times. Sometimes it will be the oceans overflowing the land, and sometimes it will be heavy rain and flooding rivers. You once had space in your societies for the animals that needed marshlands and shallow water, before levees were raised and the marshes were drained. People will help the other species to have their own living spaces.

33

Plants Create Their Growing Conditions

IT MAY SEEM that with a population of seven billion every bit of space on the planet is needed to grow food for people. The energy behind the steady expansion in human population has already changed, and will be naturally reduced in the future by way of lower birth rates and smaller families. The first noticeable reduction in the world's population will take place in the next couple of decades. The population figures at the moment are at the top of a bell curve, and they are beginning to stabilise. The way the planet is used for food will also change as people become more caring of the other life here.

The Earth is flexible, and has the ability to change dramatically. The plants and the trees live by controlling their environment, the environment does not control them. Desert plants make the air and ground dry, jungle plants bring rain. Today you live with monoculture fields that grow single crops. Seldom in nature do you find only one plant growing in a space, and even on your farms you have a constant battle to keep out unwanted plants or weeds.

Interference by man makes it harder for plants to live as they were created, to live in harmony in multi-plant neighbourhoods. The jungle is healthy and alive, while single-crop fields lack energy. Planting drifts of wild flowers in a naturalised flower bed creates a greater blend of individual energies for a healthier balance. Healthy energy creates healthy plants.

We realise that you are not used to considering plants in this manner, but then you think of them in a very simple way. Plants, when given free rein, can find their own niches. They group together and enjoy the same climate, and are replaced by new varieties as the ground becomes colder or drier. They only give trouble when lifted out of their native environments and transplanted to a new continent or location. Over time they will adjust to their new setting by accepting the current climate and the growing restrictions of the native species. These plants can be troublesome, but that will fade after a period of time. They may also influence the climate a little in their new locations. Where you see a plant out of control, it is at the beginning of its new period of adjustment and integration.

In the plant kingdom you have many allies, small living plants that want the same healthy living conditions that you do. Land plants want the right conditions for life, which includes living in natural fields of mixed crops. Can you see how that is impossible under the modern farming methods with large machinery? You could experiment by growing in fields containing a few companion crops or try new methods of farming. This will be easier if you have smaller fields and more people working the land. From a field with strips of different plants, you could move to the next step which could be inter-planting in another pattern. This isn't new information, and people who grow vegetables know they can get very good results from mixed planting. It just doesn't lend itself well to large scale mechanisation.

Growing food will continue to be a matter of concern

for humanity until the world's population begins to decline. By suggesting a change-over to mixed planting we are trying to show you a balanced method of growing greater quantities of high quality food. You will begin the process of re-populating the fields with insects and bees, birds and small wildlife. These large areas of land will slowly become healthier in themselves, and the food you eat from them will support you in health and wholeness better than current methods of growing. You can't ignore the energy present (or not present) in fields, nor can you make up for its absence in any other way as easily as by changing the way you grow crops on the land. Your farmers control their land with chemicals and machinery, and your food is an extension of these methods and is out of balance. Food is missing too many aspects of wholeness to carry vibrant and rounded energy. Would you need to eat the same quantities of food if it were of the highest quality energetically? Think about it!

In *Planet Earth Today* we wrote about a time in the future when people did not work in the fields to grow food, but food was still readily available for all. Humans would plant fruit bushes and food plants near their homes and harvest them yearly as they ripened. Until recently, all people ate in this way. They did not work to buy food, or work to grow food, they picked and ate it. At this point if you are thinking "Oh no, we're not going to become hunter-gatherers again" we want to reassure you that you have already experienced that phase of human life and do not need to repeat it, instead this would be living in a way that was new for you. The primitive hunter-gatherer tribes were not educated at universities, or familiar with art, music and science. The wage-slavery to earn the money to buy food would be gone. The money one earned would be for other items, and would be far less, and require far fewer hours to earn it. Also, for the first time in a long time, no one could tax you on the food you grew. Without fields, no one can measure how much food you've grown.

Eating fresh food makes an enormous difference to health and energy levels. The food that is manufactured, shipped and bought today has a reduced ability to sustain healthy life. Many of you simply do not know what buoyant health feels like. The poorest people who are only able to afford the cheapest food, devoid of real energy, suffer the most; their lives are often shortened because they can only afford processed food that is devoid of energy and does not maintain life force energy in their cells. Each cell is a living building block in your body and needs energy to function and reproduce. It's this energy that you are unable to see that many lack, but you recognise it when you see a person who is lively and energetic.

Earth was created as a paradise to provide you with everything you need for life, and any changes to paradise are those you made yourselves. You will tap into the energy of life when you work to change her back to fruitfulness, and that is why we see happiness in the future for those who tend her. People were designed to be strong, active and social. They recognise beauty easily with their eyes and ears, and it gives rest to their souls. What else do you need to be happy? Aligning with your natural strengths feels good and right, and leads to contentment. When you see people struggling they are often living far from their strengths and woefully off-balance. You can look forward to living balanced lives again as the decades on Earth pass by.

34

Eating Food With Energy

MANY POORER people have not learned how to cook or prepare raw food. If they bought raw food and prepared it, could they afford to buy organic food? Organic food has more energy, but not as much as wild food that is gathered and not tampered with by man in any way. We realise that gathering wild food is not a practical solution for many of you right now. You may picture tiny blackberries growing by the roadside, and wonder how many of them you would have to pick every Autumn to feed yourself. But they are a source of life energy, and that energy barely drops off even after boiling it into jam. In contrast, food that is grown in energy-less fields will never acquire additional energy after harvesting. We want you to choose the best you can for yourself according to your circumstances, this then creates a demand for better quality food to be grown. It's how you can use your money to influence the crops grown, even if the process can seem terribly slow. It's still better than the alternative, where many people don't have the energy they need for life.

In your world today there is enough food produced every day to feed your entire population and yet there is so much wastage that many go hungry. Humanity is a long way from starving as a species and the anxiety around the subject of food is misdirected. You are pushed into the arms of science to use more chemical pesticides and fertilizers or genetically modified seeds.

The recent developments around seaweed as food have the potential to unbalance the ocean ecosystems. Seaweed can be harvested, washed and eaten just as it has been for centuries, but some of the proposed seaweed farms are a replication of the giant mono-culture fields that exist on dry land. Humanity is not planning ahead on how to best utilize the growing acreage. There really is enough room and space to grow food for everyone on Earth. What has led you to you believe otherwise? It's often because food supplies have been badly disrupted by warfare in many parts of the globe. This has caused far more famine and starvation than variations in rainfall, and creates a problem that the Earth is unable to fix for you.

We write so much about food because you are physical, as well as spiritual beings. Angels are pure spirit and do not need to eat to maintain a continuous energy supply. We know we are a tiny part of the Creator, the universal source of all energy. Because we never forget this, we never lose our connection to universal life force energy. You, on the other hand, are still remembering who you are and how to connect. While you are busy remembering you need to eat to stay alive so you can continue to learn. The Earth originally provided you with everything you need for life and to connect energetically with her, and she in turn is energetically connected to the Source. She is a pure channel of this universal energy. By turning away from her and changing your growing habits, you turned away from universal energy and live impoverished, low-energy lives.

35

Ripping the Veils

STARTING over with light and fairness is an exciting
prospect! How often in your own lives have you made a
fresh start in a new direction? Small changes can get your life
moving forward again. Starting a new job or getting a divorce
are life-changing events, but they happen, and people end up
leaving the job or relationship and finding a new direction.
Humanity as a whole has started over before. After the fall of
Atlantis the human soul had a brief pause and reconfigured
its plans. While a smaller number of people continued to
live on the planet, humanity thought again about what had
gone wrong and the changes that could be made. This was
considered a fresh start having a second try at life on Earth,
and a new veil of time was erected to slow down the plans
laid by our dark angelic brothers. The dimension of time
was slowed on Earth to help contain any mistakes and allow
humanity a chance to prevent or repair problems. The fifth
dimension was hidden by the elementals at that time for
their own protection to keep them safe from human beings,
as written in *The Downfall of Atlantis*. Angels are present in
more than one dimension, and it was agreed between us
and humanity that we would step back out of sight and no
longer teach groups about the universe. It is only recently
that some humans have begun to glimpse angels once more
as the veils thin.

The thinning of the veils is important, and this is mostly

due to the changes that occurred to the Earth in 2012. Human beings are taking steps to be free of veils, and it is also time for them to dissolve now. The more some people wake up and begin to look and feel for the truth in their everyday lives and the more they struggle to see clearly, the more the veils tear. Add to this the spiritual people who are leading the way and ripping their veils one by one as they strive for the light. This helps others learn how to remove their veils, once gone very few have ever asked for them to be reinstated.

There are, of course, many who ignore veils, truth and the light and simply live their lives. They will be the last ones to follow spiritual leaders, but as all the veils begin to thin even they will start to see more and more in glimpses through the rips. Tears and rips are not just for seeing through, they allow the sensations of sight, smell, sound and emotions to enter through the holes. This will slowly change people, and by the time many of them die they will have softened a little. It will reduce the desire to kill others and despoil the Earth. Continue your work in finding the truth of who you really are.

Veils are deliberate, and were chosen to make up your blindfold as part of your game of life and ascension. The veil of time has completely vanished now for some people after they meditated and worked to accept timelessness and living in the present. Other humans that live with the veil of time, such as some of your more primitive tribes deep in a jungle, carry this veil so lightly that it is almost non-existent. It exists for them in the rising and setting of the sun and the seasons, but carries far less importance for them than the man who runs to catch a train on time. On the other hand, there are a few veils they carry very strongly. The veils are not distributed exactly evenly because of the choices you have made in how you live. You create and influence the veils, and they can be dissolved by you. No one else is going to remove your veils, but we will give what help we can.

We still teach and train those who can hear us and take our advice. These are the new leaders modelling an example for you to follow. Attend their workshops if you feel they are the right person for you. Learn from them, absorb knowledge and practice living with the light of truth.

You are able to tell truth from lies far better than you once did, do you think lies could depend on veils to obscure the truth? Lies confuse issues and distort them, are you seeing through them to the light on the other side? Use your perception to consider what politicians are telling you. We are sad that it is almost considered a necessity for politicians to lie to keep their jobs in politics. Right now you have little choice in what type of person you vote for, irregardless of party. They feel you must not know the truth or you'd interfere in how you are governed. Does this seem right to you? Join with others, dig out the truth and live together the way a soul of love deserves.

The timing to dissolve these veils is connected to the rebirth and ascension of the Earth. The rebirth changed everything, and what you are living with now is a hangover from the old Earth. Gone are veils, karma, and everyone having the opportunity to reincarnate for a new life. This was humanity's decision for the good of the human soul. Veils are irrelevant on the new Earth because you are ready to see truth without fear. And there's nothing there to be afraid of, after all.

36

Starting Over

STARTING over again is the reason humanity is still circling the sun on the new Earth. A soul of love does not need to founder in a mire of wars and killing, just as it did not have to put up with the damage to the human soul from the clones in Atlantis. Atlantis was resolved in one stroke, but you are in a different position now and can wait for the lives of those who are not really present on Earth to come to an end. All you have to do is resist any new damaging plans by speaking the truth. It's difficult to drag a child to bed when it won't come willingly; make it hard for others to drag you into their plans. As the years pass there will be changes. Just work to respect and protect the Earth as much as you can now, and protect your own soul from damage. You damage your soul when you stop treating anyone in the way you would not like to be treated yourself. There are no exceptions to this rule, and it does take some effort to live in this way. Your reward is to have an intact, whole soul.

Today you are starting over with a new plan and a future with only the souls that chose to accompany the new Earth. Humanity no longer needs everyone to have another turn at learning, because it is only repeating a few final experiences to firm them up as part of your overall soul. The individual souls that resolved to stay behind were free to do so, just as many of you choose freely to come.

Many of the souls who stayed behind have done good

work over this and previous lifetimes and are ready to rest. Others rested to be ready for this, a last period of learning and work before it is all over for good. A few decades from now, when the balance has tipped and there are far more new Earth people alive than old, it will be full steam ahead for humanity. There will be very few veils remaining to hide you from yourselves, and humans will be at their best as they connect through their hearts and interact. This is the time when you will work to make all the connections necessary for humanity's ascension, and remembering that you are all one.

Humanity is making a supreme effort to redeem a game gone wrong, and has created an ambitious and ever-changing plan. It is determined to end the game here in ascension, and not in despair. The greater human soul looked at its lack of progress and chose to pull out all the stops, throwing everything into this last chance at ascension. Your contract is with Earth; she provides the home for your game, and you pay her with respect and honour. Once humanity stopped honouring the planet it was in breach of contract and in danger of ultimate failure, and it's taken some creative thinking to work out a plan for success. How much you have learned while living on Earth!

37

Where Next?

YOU ARE living on a planet in the springtime of its new life, when it is strong and vibrant. She has ascended to another dimension and started a new existence, learning from experiences on a new level. She's learned from every guest she's ever hosted over five completely different games with completely different terrains. She has had a very hard time with you as guests, but she learned more from you than from any of the others. You came here and changed from beings of light to ungrateful houseguests, and not too surprisingly, she learned a lot in the circumstances. She learned more about light from its absence on her surface than she learned while hosting all those previous blissful games. Darkness allows the stars to shine brightly in the sky, and it allows the actions of people who strive for light to be seen. Many of you shine like stars, we can see you by your energy and you are very bright now. You who read this book are the people who did not back away, who kept up your efforts to honour the Earth.

We want you to be hopeful picturing a world that is changing rapidly following ascension. There is light here now in greater quantities than there has been on Earth for millennia, and light allows no place to hide. It's been very difficult for you to make any sense of your world while living in an impenetrable fog of lies. The fogs are being blown away, and those hiding behind masks will be exposed.

The rebirth of the Earth in 2012 and her ascension in 2015 gives humanity an incredible opportunity to reach its own ascension, by being surrounded with light. Humanity learns through the life and death cycles of those alive on Earth, and the greater human soul is busy adjusting and monitoring any opportunities to change the picture. It could not force those who are incarnate to behave in any particular way, but it has reconfigured the criteria for those who will be coming to live on Earth. In the future there will only be born the people dedicated to bringing about human ascension on the planet. Those who had the chance to go with the Earth, but declined the opportunity, will wait out the rest of this game and learn by proxy. They are not being punished, they chose to stand back or rest. Those who are being born now will mature when many old Earth residents have passed away, taking their old Earth ways of living with them, and this will speed up the process. While you wait for another generation to mature your purpose is to do the work of exposing lies, cleaning the planet and resisting those who would damage her for their own profit. That is enough work to keep you busy, and rest assured there will be more help on its way from the greater human soul.

Books by Candace Caddick

In 2009 the Archangels wanted to write a channelled book about the Earth, and help us to see the reality of the world we live on. *Planet Earth Today* shows a sentient planet of incredible beauty, and a human soul of light. I channelled this book by six Archangels, which was a combination of them explaining and me asking questions. *Planet Earth Today* is the first book of a trilogy including *The Downfall of Atlantis* and *And I Saw a New Earth* that the Archangelic Collective wrote about the coming years, while *Guidebook to the Future* is designed as a road map leading safely through the coming changes. The contents of their books are always relevant to what is happening now.

There is a single story of humanity, a golden book like a long scroll and the books have been taken from this and typed up. I felt that as long as I was learning new information when writing, information that I couldn't begin to make up, I was on track as an accurate channel. I watched the flow of golden words enter the computer each time until it was the last page of the book. After that my daughter and I checked and checked that it was written correctly, with each paragraph and line examined to see if the golden energy ran through it steadily or if it wavered indicating that it was not quite accurate. Only when we were happy was a section considered complete. Later sometimes I would add more clarity to a section, as my own understanding improved and I could put in more detail. I channel using a combination of sound and sight, and where it is written the best I have been writing down their exact words.

What they said about the books

About *Planet Earth Today:*

"The clearest message for me is: We have to act now! This book suggests gentle, effective ways to make small changes in our daily lives and help secure a bright future for humanity and for the Earth that hosts us."

DEB HOY, Editor *Touch Magazine. UK*
(available from www.reikiassociation.org.uk)

"Your book has literally changed my life – it made so much sense to me and answered so many questions I already had. I've even changed my family to organic food and products as a result! Thank you so much – it was transformational."

K GEORGE

"This clearly written, cleanly channelled book is a must for anyone willing to look at the bigger picture of Earth's history and humanity's part in her destiny."

KRISTIN BONNEY, Reiki Master UK

About *And I Saw A New Earth:*

"Although this book is an extremely 'easy read', it is one I felt needed to be taken slowly and steadily to be able to fully digest all the fascinating and encouraging information within its pages. With each chapter being devoted to a particular subject, this book answers many questions whilst opening up new perspectives for the reader to explore. One of the best channelled works I have seen – it has certainly given me much on which to ponder."

JOAN OSBORNE, *Paradigm Shift Magazine* March 2013

Planet Earth Today

The first book gives background information on the roles of Earth and the human soul in the universe. Life is experienced so that we can know ourselves and learn why we are alive. Humanity wished to live on Earth wearing a blindfold; we could see neither the higher dimensions or connect to our greater human soul. This led to great loneliness and separation as we began to play the hardest game ever conceived. The Archangel of Darkness presents his point of view of humanity on Earth, and the Archangels of Light Ariel, Esmariel, and Hophriel write with techniques to take us forward with hope.

This book serves as the introduction to the trilogy as it takes place before the other two books in time, and the information there about the planet or Atlantis is not repeated in any other book. However, each book stands alone and can be read individually.

ISBN 978-0-9565009-0-8

The Downfall of Atlantis

In the story of humanity on Earth, the time spent living and learning on Atlantis cannot be ignored. During those long years the darkness gathered around human beings, and science developed a heartless approach. There were slaves made of combinations of animals and people and ultimately cloning to keep the wealthy and important alive indefinitely. Cloning was the final crack in the system that led to ruin and the end of Atlantis.

Those who refused to go along with the new science escaped the end and settled on the surrounding land masses forming the new post-Atlantean civilisations. The Atlantean influence is explored in the cultures of Africa, Egypt, Britain and Celtic Europe, North, Central and South America. They learned much from these people in return.

Atlantean civilisation remained intact for a long time in Britain because of the ancient sites of power at Avebury, Stonehenge and Glastonbury Tor. When the Shadow in the East pushed westwards into Europe the light of these venerable societies vanished until only (the now mythical) King Arthur and Merlin were left to protect the Earth from darkness. Their story explains the true significance of the great stone circles, and how we came to forget the real story of Arthur and the sacrifices he made to destroy the invading armies. The connection in a straight line between Atlantis, post-Atlantean civilisations, King Arthur and the Time of Legends is explored so we can remember those things we have forgotten, and not repeat past mistakes.

ISBN 978-0-9565009-1-5

And I Saw A New Earth

Humanity is entering its golden years, when we begin to live as we always intended when we came to Earth. It will be like breathing for the first time, the sweet fresh air that is real life filled with joy, truth and clear-sightedness. *And I Saw A New Earth* is a channelled book about light, written by those who have ascended in wisdom and understanding and wish to help during a time of rapid change.

During 2012 the Earth received wave after wave of light, enough light to change the way we relate to each other, enough light to show us the lies that have kept us from living in joy. By December the rebirth of Earth herself took place filled with the energy of Spring and fresh beginnings. Humanity can use this energy to remove the institutions that failed to work, and restore the balance between work and play. 2012 ended the world we know: one of gross inequality and lack of hope. The coming years give us the chance to build societies of love and fairness, and leave behind the institutions that failed us.

And I Saw a New Earth is written to reassure us that we can trust our intuition and our hearts, and that our real future lies ahead for us to enjoy. Humanity has one of the most important roles in the future of the universe.

ISBN: 978-0-9565009-2-2

Guidebook to the Future

There are an overwhelming number of changes taking place in the coming years. It's as if we began a long journey without a map where the road, even the destination, keeps changing while we travel. As soon as we become accustomed to one change another one takes its place. It's the beginning of the new 26,000 year galactic cycle and of the new Earth. Changes are taking place in the higher dimensions that will affect our societies and economies and influence the forward progress of humanity. Think of this book as a map or guidebook into the future, showing us the new energy and how it shapes our individual pathways. We can relax, let go and enjoy the journey.

Angels are beings of love and light, and this book was channelled to help people look past the radical new changes to the happier world beyond.

ISBN: 978-0-9565009-3-9

Books available from online retailers.

About the Author

I am a teaching Reiki Master who studied for ten years with my Master, prior to initiation in the Usui Shiki Ryoho system of Reiki. Since 1993 I have been practicing my own Reiki daily and my ability to channel has become clearer and stronger until a few years ago I realised I was able to see the world around me in a way that others did not. My efforts, as I worked with my own archangelic guides as a channel, were always to unblock and deliver the message clearly, with no preconceptions of what they may say next; to stand well back and just watch and listen.

Before learning Reiki I trained as an economist, worked inside the United States Congress in Washington D.C. as a legislative assistant, and retrained as a nutritionist in the UK.

If you want to read more from the Archangels and other beings of light, I write a regular channelled blog at:

www.candacecaddick.com

www.ingramcontent.com/pod-product-compliance
Lightning Source LLC
Chambersburg PA
CBHW032046090426
42744CB00004B/103